WHAT BECAME OF PETER'S DREAM?

DISTRIBUTED BY UNIVERSITY OF WASHINGTON PRESS

SEATTLE AND LONDON

What Became of Peter's Dream?

COURT CULTURE IN THE REIGN OF NICHOLAS II

ANNE ODOM

WITH AN INTRODUCTION BY

RICHARD SAUNDERS

MIDDLEBURY COLLEGE MUSEUM OF ART · VERMONT

HILLWOOD MUSEUM AND GARDENS · WASHINGTON, D.C.

This catalogue accompanies the exhibition
What Became of Peter's Dream? Court Culture in the Reign of Nicholas II,
on view at the Middlebury College Museum of Art from
September 19 through December 7, 2003.

Published by Middlebury College Museum of Art, Middlebury, Vermont,
and Hillwood Museum and Gardens, Washington, D.C.

Distributed by University of Washington Press, Seattle

Library of Congress Number: 2003105594

ISBN 1-928825-03-6

Edited by Nancy Eickel
Designed by Christopher Kuntze
Printed in Iceland by Oddi Printing

PHOTOGRAPHY CREDITS
Ken Burris: Figs. 14, 19, 20, 23–25, 27–29, 34, cats. 45, 53, 55, 75
Edward Owen: Cover and frontispiece, figs. 1–13, 15–18,
21, 22, 26, 31–33, 35–37, cats. 31, 76, 93, 95
Jack Abraham: Figs. 38, 39

COVER DETAIL AND FRONTISPIECE
Bread and salt dish, 1894–96. A. Glazunova, painter. Faience.
Hillwood Museum and Gardens (fig. 10, cat. 12)

CONTENTS

FOREWORD

Hillwood Museum and Gardens in Washington, D.C., the former home of Marjorie Merriweather Post, houses the largest collection of imperial Russian fine and decorative arts outside Russia. This distinguished exhibition dovetails perfectly with one of our museum's strategic goals: to collaborate with academic institutions in an effort to acquaint a broader audience with our splendid collections. Middlebury College, where Russian language and studies have long been part of the curriculum, is an ideal partner in such a venture.

I am indebted to Anne Odom, Hillwood's Curator Emerita, for her discerning scholarship that is so well presented in this handsomely designed catalogue. Anne continues to bring new thinking to the growing literature in the field of Russian decorative arts. She has been instrumental in establishing Hillwood's publishing program, and she has contributed numerous important books and articles on Russia's arts. I also want to thank and congratulate Richard Saunders, Director of Middlebury's Museum of Art, for his vision of this wonderful undertaking. Finally, I want to express my gratitude to Emmie Donadio, Associate Director of Middlebury's Museum of Art, for all of her efforts in making this project a reality.

Frederick J. Fisher
Executive Director
Hillwood Museum and Gardens

NOTES TO THE READER & ACKNOWLEDGMENTS

A modified Library of Congress transliteration system has been used in this book. Soft signs have been omitted except in the footnotes. The names of the tsars and tsarinas have been used in their Western form. All others have been rendered in their Russian form, including Grand Duke Georgii Mikhailovich, usually known as Grand Duke George in the West, and his wife, Maria Georgievna, often referred to as Grand Duchess George or Princess Marie of Greece. One exception has been Xenia (Ksenia), one of Georgii's daughters, who lived almost her entire life in the West. Nicholas II's sister Kseniia is spelled in the Russian manner. Several other Russian names, such as Carl Fabergé and Alexander Benois, are also used in their Western form.

A first name and patronymic is the polite way of referring to all Russians. Georgii Mikhailovich means that Georgii is the son of Mikhail.

If the events occurred in Russia, the dates used are in the old style. Russians used the Julian calendar until 1917, which in the twentieth century is thirteen days behind the Gregorian calendar used in the West. Any Western dates are indicted by "N.S." for new style.

I would like to thank the many people who have read the manuscript, shared ideas, and helped locate nagging bits of information. I am indebted to Elena Harbick and Kristen Regina at Hillwood, and especially Wendy Salmond and my husband, Bill Odom, for reading the manuscript and for their many valuable suggestions. Hays Browning receives my thanks for compiling a complicated genealogy. I am grateful to Middlebury College for the opportunity to work on this exhibition. Director Richard Saunders, Emmie Donadio, and Meg Wallace have been unfailingly helpful. I would particularly like to thank Hillwood's director, Frederick Fisher, and the Board of Directors of the Marjorie Merriweather Post Foundation of D.C. for their support of this project.

Anne Odom

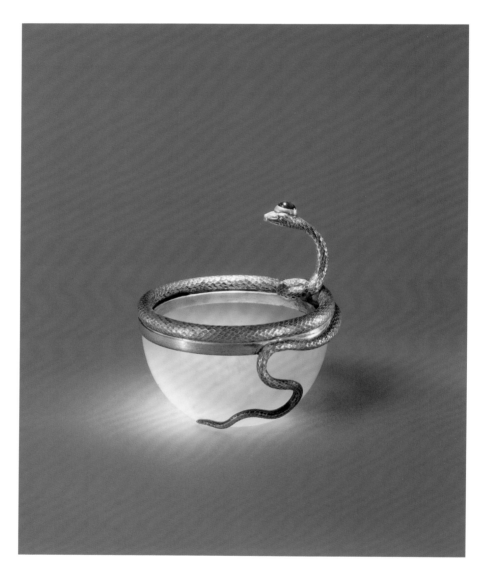

Cat. 45. Bowl, early 20th century. Silver gilt, bowenite, ruby
Middlebury College Museum of Art, Gift of Nancy and Edward Wynkoop

INTRODUCTION

In 1993 a potential donor to the art collection of Middlebury College made us a remarkable offer. If it could be kept together, an early twentieth-century family collection of some one hundred decorative art objects made by Russian silversmiths and jewelers—including Carl Fabergé and his workshop—might eventually come to the Museum. Middlebury College, with its substantial programs in Russian language and Russian and east European studies, seemed a perfect repository for the collection. We had recently opened a new Center for the Arts building, and we were interested in expanding our art collection. Furthermore, this was no ordinary group of objects: it had belonged to a branch of the Romanov family. Its extraordinary survival—from pre-revolutionary Russia to Woodstock, Vermont—carried a fascinating history of its own, and its record of ownership as objects crafted by Fabergé was a decisive asset. Few collections of this size and with such a family provenance still survived intact.

Nancy Leeds Wynkoop and her husband Edward are the generous donors of this collection of objects that came through her mother Xenia, the daughter of Grand Duke Georgii Mikhailovich and his wife, Grand Duchess Maria Georgievna (Princess Marie of Greece and Denmark). Each of her mother's parents was in turn a direct descendant of Nicholas I. Nancy's grandfather was one of the five sons of Mikhail Nikolaevich, the youngest of the tsar's sons. He and two of his brothers were assassinated at the Peter and Paul Fortress in Petrograd on 30 January 1919. Nancy's grandmother Maria was also a granddaughter of Grand Duke Konstantin Nikolaevich, one of Mikhail's older brothers. Both of Nancy's maternal grandparents, therefore, were first cousins once removed of the last reigning Romanov tsar, Nicholas II. (See the family tree on page 15.)

While Nancy's grandmother Maria, daughter of King George of the Hellenes, and Olga, daughter of Grand Duke Konstantin, had grown up in Greece, her grandfather, Grand Duke Georgii Mikhailovich, came from Tbilisi in the Caucasus. As a young man he had been interested in painting. His family frowned upon this notion and insisted that its men pursue military careers. In later years he served as director of the Alexander III Museum in Petersburg (now the State Russian Museum), established by his cousin Nicholas II in 1898. The grand duke also had an avid interest in numismatics and wrote several monographs on the subject. What was salvaged of his own remarkably comprehensive Russian coin collection was brought to his widow and is now in the Smithsonian Institution.[1] When they married and for six years thereafter, Georgii and Maria lived in St. Petersburg in the New Mikhailovskii Palace, the residence of Georgii's father, Grand Duke Mikhail. Xenia and her sister Nina were born there. Soon, however, the couple established another residence in the Caucasus, giving it the Greek name Harax (to the delight of Maria); many of the objects in the Middlebury collection originated from there.

Among these prized objects is a picture frame that marks the tenth anniversary of the grand duke and his wife in 1910. Within its shape—the Roman numeral ten—are images of Georgii Mikhailovich and his daughters Nina and Xenia (fig. 23). Also in the collection are other picture frames with images of family members, demonstrating a love of both family photographs and the luxury items to feature them. These picture frames, cigarette cases, figurines, desk accessories, silver service, and other bibelots form the bulk of Middlebury's collection. In a letter to the Museum in 1994, Nancy Wynkoop noted their connection to her ancestors and called the objects her "beloved treasures" because she had "great love for them having grown up with most of them." These works, most of them small and suitable for setting out on bureaus, table tops, and desks, were exchanged on birthdays, anniversaries, and important religious occasions. They served as reminders of the vital and loving relationships among members of the Romanov family. Today they offer poignant glimpses of the taste and customs of the Russian imperial family.

The survival of the collection now at Middlebury is owed to two women of the family. Olga, Queen of Greece (and grandmother of Xenia), saved many of the Fabergé objects when she left Russia. The Dowager Empress Maria Fedorovna, mother of Nicholas II, brought most of the silver service with her in 1919, when her nephew, King George V of England, ordered the Admiralty to rescue her by warship.[2] Maria and her daughters were spared Grand Duke Georgii Mikhailovich's fate of assassination because they had left Russia for England in the summer of 1914. When World War I broke out that year, they were guests of King George V in Buckingham Palace. What had begun as an excursion of indefinite length became a permanent exodus. The memoirs of Nancy's grandmother include letters that Georgii Mikhailovich

---

1. David Chachavadze, *The Grand Dukes* (New York: Atlantic International Publications, 1990), 184.

2. John Curtis Perry and Constantine Pleshakov, *The Flight of the Romanovs: A Family Saga* (New York, Basic Books, 1999), 217.

Cat. 55. Triptych frame, ca. 1908. Firm of Fabergé, Viktor Aarne, workmaster
Gold, enamel, pearls, diamond, miniatures on ivory
Middlebury College Museum of Art, Gift of Nancy and Edward Wynkoop

wrote to his wife while he was imprisoned in Vologda before his assassination in 1919.[3]

While Middlebury is fortunate indeed to have access to this extraordinarily rich legacy, we are equally fortunate in our association with Anne Curtis Odom, College alumna and Curator Emerita of Hillwood Museum and Gardens in Washington, D.C. Since our first meeting with Nancy and Edward Wynkoop, Anne has alerted us to the significance and the fascinating history of these surviving artifacts. It has long been our hope that we might present this collection in a context adequate to its historical worth, and Anne's enthusiasm for the project and her extensive knowledge have inspired and informed us all. Thanks to Anne and to the Hillwood Museum, its director Frederick J. Fisher, and its trustees, we are now able to realize that dream. We gratefully acknowledge the generosity of spirit, of scholarship and knowledge, and finally of funding that Hillwood has made possible. This exhibition and publication would not exist without that support.

In addition to the extraordinary contribution of essential works from the Hillwood collection, Anne has been able to secure loans from private collections, from Set Charles Momjian, and from the Jane Voorhees Zimmerli Art Museum, Rutgers, The State University of New Jersey. We thank these lenders, in addition to the Wynkoops, for making it possible for us to provide a fully adequate historical and aesthetic context for our own precious objects.

About three years ago we realized in conversations with Anne that the three hundredth anniversary of the founding of St. Petersburg would be a perfect occasion on which to build an exhibition. Since the objects in our collection relate to the reign of Nicholas II, we decided to focus on the city's two hundredth anniversary. Thus *What Became of Peter's Dream? Court Culture in the Reign of Nicholas II* has been an opportunity for us to reflect upon the last centennial and to use hindsight to distinguish among the various strands of cultural history that appear most salient, if foreboding, today.

An installation of selected works from the Wynkoops has been on public view at Middlebury periodically in past years, and for their ongoing efforts to research and present these objects I thank Monica McCabe, former collections manager; Christine Fraioli, Museum consultant; and Kenneth Pohlman, Museum designer. Alice Illich, formerly of Christie's, London, has also been

---

3. Grand Duchess George, *A Romanov Diary. The Autobiography of H.I. and R.H. Grand Duchess George* (New York: Atlantic International Publications, 1988).

12

of great assistance to the Museum. Meg Wallace, our indefatigable registrar who also serves as publications consultant, has played a major role in every phase of this project. Another debt of gratitude goes to Emmie Donadio, associate director of the Museum, who as acting director in 1989 was first contacted about the possibility of exhibiting the Wynkoop collection. Since that time Emmie has worked devotedly on the project. She has interviewed and corresponded with Nancy on the history of the collection, and with Anne she has labored to produce this publication. For additional assistance I also acknowledge the efforts of Clarence "Bud" Leeds and Michael Schoenfeld.

The generosity of the Christian A. Johnson Endeavor Foundation and the far-sighted philanthropy of Julie Johnson Kidd have facilitated the Museum's projects over the years. At the same time the Middlebury College Arts Council, founded in 1998, of which Anne Odom is also a member, is to be thanked for its essential contribution to our efforts.

Without a doubt our largest debt of gratitude goes to Nancy and Edward Wynkoop for caring for these treasures, assuring their safety and security, and allowing them to come to Middlebury so that future generations can enjoy their beauty and learn the lessons they have to offer.

Richard Saunders
Director, Middlebury College Museum of Art
Walter Cerf Distinguished College Professor

I The Romanov Dynasty 1613–1917 (Reign Dates)

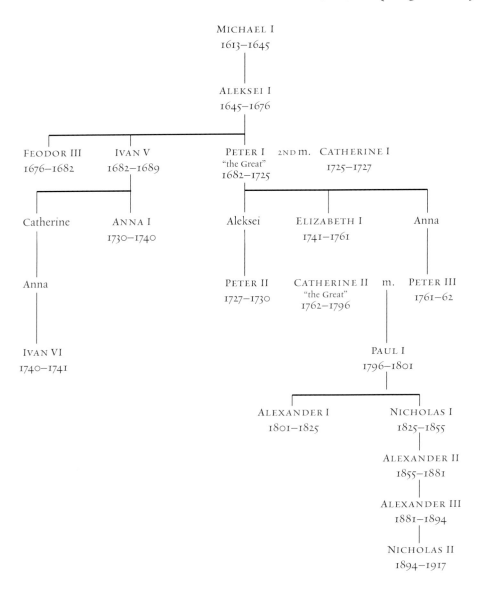

MICHAEL I
1613–1645

ALEKSEI I
1645–1676

FEODOR III
1676–1682

IVAN V
1682–1689

PETER I
"the Great"
1682–1725

2ND m.

CATHERINE I
1725–1727

Catherine

ANNA I
1730–1740

Aleksei

ELIZABETH I
1741–1761

Anna

Anna

PETER II
1727–1730

CATHERINE II
"the Great"
1762–1796

m.

PETER III
1761–62

IVAN VI
1740–1741

PAUL I
1796–1801

ALEXANDER I
1801–1825

NICHOLAS I
1825–1855

ALEXANDER II
1855–1881

ALEXANDER III
1881–1894

NICHOLAS II
1894–1917

II ROMANOV RELATIONSHIPS

NICHOLAS I, Tsar 1825–1855 m. Alexandra Fedorovna of Prussia, 1798–1860

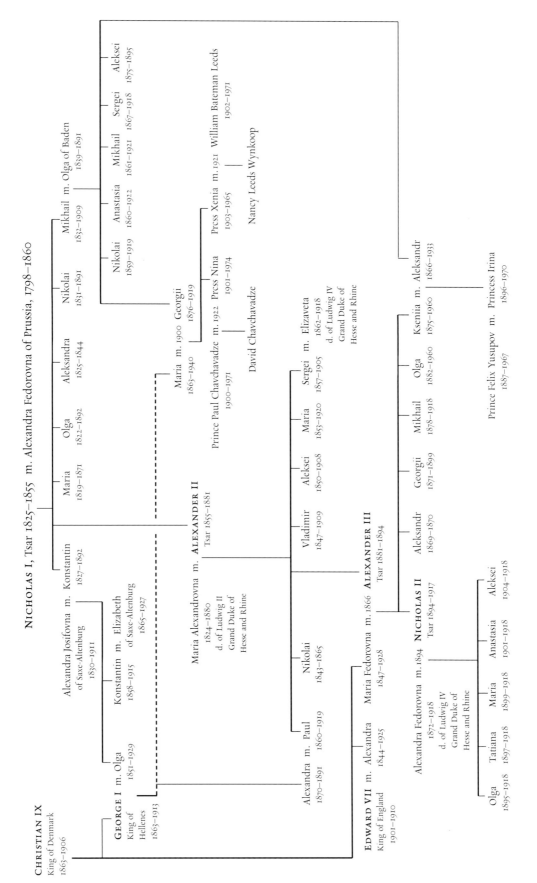

Romanov Dynasty Genealogies compiled by Hays R. Browning

Fig. 1. Detail of coronation menu, 1896
Colored lithograph after a drawing by Viktor Vasnetsov
Hillwood Museum and Gardens (cat. 10)

What Became of Peter's Dream?
COURT CULTURE IN THE REIGN OF NICHOLAS II

T HE YEAR 1903 marked the bicentenary of the founding of St. Petersburg. This should have been the year to celebrate Peter the Great and his beautiful Western city, the Venice of the North, the Northern Palmyra. Several of the most memorable events, however, would have stood at odds with Peter's dream. The Winter Ball, now usually referred to as the Boyar Ball, Russia's grandest social event in many years, was held in the Winter Palace that February. All the guests, including not only all members of the imperial family but also the leading aristocrats, officers of the imperial guards regiments, and high-ranking officials, were requested to appear in the historical costume of the boyars, the old Russian aristocracy, and other pre-Petrine ranks of the seventeenth century—indeed, the very attire that Peter had rejected in favor of Western dress. Emperor Nicholas arrived in a copy of a court robe worn by Peter's father, Tsar Aleksei Mikhailovich (fig. 2), and Alexandra appeared as Maria Miloslavskaia, Aleksei's first wife (fig. 3). Alexandra designed her own costume and that of her husband with the help of Ivan Vsevolozhskii, director of the Hermitage.[1]

Members of the court sought out ancient costumes and wore heirloom jewels. The aunt of the famous Russian-American novelist Vladimir Nabokov wore a costume designed by the impresario Sergei Diagilev. She provided the firm of Carl Fabergé with her own jewels to be used in the decoration of her *kokoshnik* (a traditional Russian headdress) and *barma*, the large embroidered yoke that went around her neck.[2] Maria Georgievna (fig. 4), the wife of Grand Duke Georgii Mikhailovich (fig. 5), remembered that "some mysterious magic seemed to have changed all these familiar figures into splendid visions out of Russia's oriental past."[3] The 1903 ball, the last one held in the Winter Palace,

1. Baroness Sophie Buxhoeveden, *The Life and Tragedy of Alexandra Feodorovna. Empress of Russia. A Biography* (London: Longmans, Green and Company, 1930; reprint 1996), 98.

2. Nadine Wonlar-Larsky, *The Russia that I Loved* (London: Elsie MacSwinney Trants, 1937; reprint 1952), 98. Grand Duchess Kseniia, Nicholas's sister, ordered from Fabergé a fan of ostrich feathers with a rock crystal handle mounted in enamel and gold. It is now in the Forbes Magazine Collection in New York. See Alexander von Solodkoff, *Masterpieces from the House of Fabergé* (New York: Harry N. Abrams, 1984), 30.

3. *A Romanov Diary, An Autobiography of H.I. and R.H. Grand Duchess George* (New York: Atlantic International Publications, 1988), 103.

Fig. 2. Nicholas II in the costume of Tsar Aleksei Mikhailovich. Photogravure from a photograph by Levitskii, 1903. *Al'bom kostiumirovannago bala*. Hillwood Museum and Gardens Art Library, Dunning Collection (cat. 4a)

Fig. 3. Alexandra Fedorovna in the costume of Maria Miloslavskaia. Photogravure from a photograph by Levitskii, 1903. *Al'bom kostiumirovannago bala*. Hillwood Museum and Gardens Art Library, Dunning Collection (cat. 4b)

represents Nicholas's growing fascination for an ideal Russia based on the seventeenth century. As his brother-in-law Aleksandr Mikhailovich said, "For at least one night Nicky wanted to be back in the glorious past of our family."[4] Nicholas does not seem to have been satisfied with just a grand masquerade ball. According to Aleksandr Mosolov, head of the Chancellery of the Ministry

---

4. Alexander, Grand Duke of Russia, *Once a Grand Duke* (New York: Farrar and Rinehart, 1932), 211.

Fig. 4. Grand Duchess Maria Georgievna in the costume of a peasant woman from Torzhok. Photogravure from a photograph by Boissonas and F. Eggler, 1903. *Al'bom kostiumirovanna-go bala.* Hillwood Museum and Gardens Art Library, Dunning Collection (cat. 4c)

Fig. 5. Grand Duke Georgii Mikhailovich in the costume of a seventeenth-century boyar. Photogravure from a photograph by Levitskii, 1903. *Al'bom kostiumirovannago bala.* Hillwood Museum and Gardens Art Library, Dunning Collection (cat. 4d)

of the Court, Nicholas even considered restoring Muscovite court dress. He had designs drawn up, but soon found the plan to be too expensive.[5]

This throwback to the spirit of Moscovy was not limited to fashion. In that same year Nicholas II once again spent Easter, one of the most important celebrations in the Russian calendar, in Moscow, as he had been doing since

---

5. A.A. Mosolov, *Pri dvore poslednego imperatora. Zapiski nachal'nika kantseliarii ministerstva dvora* (St. Petersburg: Nauka, 1992), 84.

1900. There, among the great religious monuments of the Kremlin, Nicholas was moved by the presence of God, and he enjoyed a special unity with the people, something he did not experience in St. Petersburg.[6] Furthermore, in July, Nicholas and Alexandra went to Sarov to participate in the glorification (the Orthodox equivalent of a canonization) of Serafim of Sarov in the fervent hope that their prayers on this occasion would bring them a son and heir. Saint Serafim was a monk saint, whose glorification Nicholas and Alexandra encouraged and who came to hold tremendous significance for the couple after the birth of Tsarevich Aleksei in 1904.

On the two hundredth anniversary of St. Petersburg's founding, what had become of Peter's dream to create not only a new city that would be a "window on the West" but also a new culture? What had happened to Peter's great expectations for St. Petersburg and Westernization? In fact, the extensive celebrations—"the long awaited 'Peter Week'"—began on 16 May, the date on which Peter is supposed to have founded the city.[7] On that day, following an eight o'clock salute from the Peter and Paul Fortress, the imperial party sailed down the Neva from Peter's *Domik*, the first house he built in the city. Members of the group participated in a service at St. Isaac's Cathedral, attended a ceremony at the famous statue of Peter by Etienne-Maurice Falconet, and placed medals struck in Peter's honor on his grave at the Cathedral of Peter and Paul. Throughout the week the city was lavishly decorated. Exhibits, illuminations, and yacht races were held in Peter's honor, along with grand banquets for foreign visitors. Nicholas must have endured these ceremonies out of necessity, having noted that he liked Peter less than his other ancestors due to "his fascination for western culture and his scorn for all pure Russian customs."[8] The elaborate festivities and fine weather seemed to have had no impact on the numerous memoirists who wrote voluminously about the Boyar Ball and the glorification of Saint Serafim, for they failed to mention this historic moment.

These events and attitudes reveal the ambivalence and the tensions that existed between Muscovite Russia and Peter's Westernized Russia, which are often symbolized by the two cities—Moscow and St. Petersburg. Nicholas himself inhabited these two worlds simultaneously. He lived a totally West-

---

6. Richard Wortman, "Moscow and Petersburg: The Problem of Political Center in Tsarist Russia, 1881–1914," in *Rites of Power: Symbolism, Ritual and Politics since the Middle Ages*, ed. Sean Willentz (Philadelphia: University of Pennsylvania Press, 1985), 262.

7. *Niva*, vols. 19, 20, 21 (1903). In addition to *Niva*, *Khudozhestvennye sokrovishcha Rossii*, vol. 3 (1903), featured artifacts, portraits, and engravings from the time of Peter.

8. Mosolov, 80.

ern life in St. Petersburg in surroundings more English than Russian, and in his early years he often traveled to western Europe. Increasingly, however, he sought refuge from the strains of ruling over a modern society by turning to his romantic view of the reign of Tsar Aleksei, Peter's father, which he considered to have been a peaceful period of harmonious relations between tsar and people. The Boyar Ball symbolized that retreat. He believed that the birth of his son Aleksei, whom he named after his favorite ancestor, was a miracle wrought by Saint Serafim of Sarov. This conviction gave him confidence that God would reveal the way in future decisions and that whatever happened was God's will. Increasingly, Nicholas was living in a hermetically sealed world, one isolated from the reality of Peter's dream, which was actually alive and thriving.

The applied arts produced during Nicholas II's reign serve as a reliable reflection of these conflicting worlds because they are directly related not only to ceremony but also to everyday life. They mirror the fashions of the elite as well as the rising middle class. The objects discussed here help us to focus on these obvious tensions between Peter's dream in 1703 and the founding of the Romanov dynasty in 1613, the very tradition that Peter had hoped to eradicate. Through them we can gain a more complete picture of court culture at the time of Nicholas II, but peripherally we can also view the extraordinarily rich and increasingly diverse bourgeois culture that was growing and would make the last two decades of imperial Russia worthy of the name "the Silver Age." The newly emerging merchants and industrialists financed and collected the work of a variety of artists. The World of Art, an innovative movement under the energetic leadership of Diagilev, aspired to reinvigorate and strengthen links with the West and forge a new dialogue. Numerous groups contributed to the rich visual culture that existed during the reign of Nicholas II.

The central theme of this essay, however, revolves around the court, its ceremony, and the life of the imperial family. Despite the decline of its power, the artistic legacy of the tsar's court was significant and is still wildly popular as we celebrate the three hundredth anniversary of the founding of St. Petersburg.

WHAT WAS PETER'S DREAM?

The expansion of luxury industries in the eighteenth century was a fundamental part of the modernization of all European monarchies. As historian Peter Burke has written, "Ritual, art and architecture [and we might also add the decorative arts] may all be seen as the instruments of self-assertion, as the continuation of war and diplomacy by other means."[9] The modernization of European societies was well under way in the Netherlands and Britain when Peter the Great (r. 1682–1725) came to the throne. He surely perceived the dynamics of modernization when he embarked in 1697 on the Grand Embassy, a two-year tour of Europe that made a lasting impression on him. The sights he saw certainly fueled the ambition in this young man, who had already been exposed to Western culture in the German quarter of Moscow. The trip heightened his desire to leave the Byzantine and Asiatic ways of Muscovite Russia far behind him.

Peter's most compelling reason to modernize the state he now ruled was military. Continually at war with the Turks and soon to be at war with the Swedes, Peter required more advanced weapons and a better-educated officer corps to defeat these powerful enemies. What he must have appreciated on his travels was the concept that Russia also needed to Westernize its "theater of power" if it was going to be anything but an insignificant bystander on the periphery of Europe. A successful army would give Russia the prestige it needed to be taken seriously by Western nations, but the "theater of power" required all the baggage of modern eighteenth-century civilization: education, scientific inquiry, efficient government, the arts, theater, and literature.[10]

This "theater," called by another author "the theater of self-presentation,"[11] was enacted most successfully on the occasions of coronations, dynastic marriages, military victories, and official visits. At those times princely hosts utilized parades, triumphal arches, grand banquets, fireworks, and illuminations as a form of advertisement, hoping that all the visitors would spread far and wide word of the magnificence of their courts.[12] The arts played a critical role in these opulent demonstrations of power. Grand ceremony had existed for centuries in both the East and West, but the trappings that constituted

---

9. Quoted in T.C.W. Blanning, *The Culture of Power and the Power of Culture. Old Regime Europe 1660–1789* (Oxford: Oxford University Press, 2002), 5.

10. Richard S. Wortman uses the term "theater of power" throughout his work *Scenarios of Power. Myth and Ceremony in Russian Monarchy*, vols. 1 and 2 (Princeton: Princeton University Press, 1995 and 2000). Simon Dixon, in *Catherine the Great* (Harlow, England: Longman, 2001), 48–53, refers to the court as Catherine's "theater of power."

11. Thomas DaCosta Kaufman, *Court, Cloister and City. The Art and Culture of Central Europe 1450–1800* (Chicago: University of Chicago Press, 1995), 308.

12. For more on the phenomenon of royal propaganda, see John Adamson, ed., *Princely Courts of Europe: Ritual, Politics and Culture under the Ancien Regime 1500–1750* (London: Seven Dials, Cassell, 2000), 33–35.

ceremonial power had changed in the course of the seventeenth century. The acknowledged leader in this new game was Louis XIV of France, with his complicated court etiquette, sumptuously decorated palace, and beautifully manicured gardens at Versailles. Russians, who already appreciated the power of splendor, realized they would have to adopt this Western version if they were to be accepted into the European community.[13]

Architectural monuments and gardens were the most obvious component in this "theater of self-presentation," and although they have received the most scholarly attention, they were not the only indicator of cultural influence. Increasingly critical was the ruler's display of his native products—everything from the silks and tapestries on the walls to the furniture, the silver and, in the course of the eighteenth century, the porcelain on the table. Locally made luxury wares demonstrated the technical and artistic sophistication of a prince's realm. They also reduced the need to import costly goods from abroad.

If architecture was one of the first outward symbols of a monarch's modernization, then constructing a brand new city provided the perfect opportunity to realize a modern vision. Peter immediately hired various architects to design his "window on the West." They included Domenico Trezzini, a Swiss-Italian working in Copenhagen, who arrived in Russia in 1703 and built the first Winter Palace and the Cathedral of Saints Peter and Paul; Jean-Baptiste-Alexandre Le Blond, a student of André Le Nôtre, who in 1716 laid out plans for Vasilevskii Island and the palace and gardens at Peterhof; and Georg Johann Mattarnovi, who designed the Kunstkamera and the second Winter Palace.

Peter also sought out Western artists, such as Gottfried Kneller, who painted the Russian leader's portrait in 1698 while he was in London, and Charles Boit, who based several miniatures on the Kneller portrait. The emperor used these small portraits to reward deserving servants of the state.[14] He invited others to Russia, including the German artist Johann Gottfried Tannauer (also Dannhauer) (fig. 6) and Louis Caravaque, whom he hired in 1716 to paint historical pictures, the most important of which was of Peter at the Battle of Poltava. Peter did not neglect Russian artists, however. In 1711 he ordered the most accomplished artists and artisans in Moscow's Kremlin Armory workshops transferred to St. Petersburg.

---

13. For a pre-Petrine appreciation of ceremony, see Anzhella G. Kudriavtseva, "Ambassadorial Ceremony at the Tsar's Court," in *Gifts to the Tsars 1500–1700. Treasures from the Kremlin*, edited by Barry Shifman and Guy Walton (New York: Harry N. Abrams, 2001), 43–61.

14. See Christie's, New York, 19 October 2001, lot 91, for one of the miniatures painted by Boit.

PETRVS   MAGNVS
TOTIVS RVSSIÆ   IMPERATOR
ET AVTO-   -CRATOR
PATER   PATRIÆ

Fig. 6. *Peter the Great*. Engraving after Johann Gottfried Tannauer, 1714.
The George Riabov Collection of Russian Art, Jane Voorhees Zimmerli Art Museum,
Rutgers, The State University of New Jersey (cat. 1)

Although he lived simply and was often in the field, Peter was not averse to luxury, and he understood the critical role silver played in grand ceremonial dining. He ordered a silver service for twenty-four persons in 1711.[15] Within the next three years foreign silversmiths in St. Petersburg formed a guild following Western standards. Peter officially recognized it in 1721, and the following year a guild of Russian silversmiths was established.[16]

Expensive tapestries had long been used to display personal wealth and refined taste.[17] On a second trip to Europe in 1716 and 1717, shortly after Louis XIV's death, Peter visited Versailles and the Gobelins Factory. This inspired him to establish the Imperial Tapestry Factory, operated by weavers from Gobelins who were under the supervision of Le Blond.[18] According to their contracts, foreign weavers were required to train Russians, and by the end of the century most of the court's weavers were natives. The disproportionate role assigned to luxury industries in Peter's economy is revealed in a comment made by one nineteenth-century visitor: "It is characteristic of Russia . . . that it had founded a tapestry manufactory before it could spin cotton."[19]

Peter was also intent upon competing with his fellow monarchs to create a porcelain factory. The mania for porcelain exploded in the seventeenth century with the increased importation of Chinese and Japanese porcelains into Europe. Peter himself purchased through the East India Company more than five hundred pieces for Monplaisir alone, his small pavilion at Peterhof.[20] For their display, he commissioned Hendrick van Brumkorst, a Dutchman and one of the first foreign craftsmen to work in St. Petersburg, to install an exquisite lacquer cabinet. This tiny display area was surely inspired by the fashionable rooms paneled with Chinese lacquer and used to show off rare Chinese porcelains that Peter had seen on his travels in Europe.[21]

---

15. Z.A. Berniakovich, *Russkoe khudozhestvennoe serebro XVIII-nachala XX veka* (Leningrad: Khudozhnik RSFSR, 1977), 8. Nothing from this service, which Peter stipulated should be "plain and without decoration or gilding," seems to survive. At the beginning of the twentieth century only two tureens remained in the Hermitage. See Baron A.E. Fel'kersam, *Opisi serebra dvora Ego Imperatorskago Velichestva* (St. Petersburg: R. Golike and A. Vil'borg, 1907), vol. 1, pl. 23, and vol. 2, 506–507.

16. M.M. Postnikova-Loseva, N.G. Platonova, and B.L. Ul'ianova, *Zolotoe i serebrianoe delo XV–XXvv* (Moscow: Nauka, 1983), 123–24.

17. See Thomas P. Campbell, *Tapestry in the Renaissance: Art and Magnificence* (New York: Metropolitan Museum of Art and Yale University Press, 2002), 15.

18. T.T. Korshunova, *Russkie shpalery: Peterburg. shpalernaia manufaktura* (Leningrad: Khudozhnik RSFSR, 1975), 34.

19. J.G. Kohl, esq., *Russia and the Russians*, vol. 1 (Philadelphia: Carey and Hart, 1843), 116.

20. T. Arapova and T.V. Kudriavtseva, *Dal'nevostochnyi farfor v Rossii XVIII-nachalo XX veka* (St. Petersburg: AO Slaviia-Interbuk, 1994), 4.

21. I.N. Ukhanova, "G. Brumkhorst—Peterburgskii master lakovogo dela," *Kul'tura i iskusstvo petrovskogo vremeni* (Leningrad: State Hermitage, 1977), 174–82.

Importing porcelain proved to be expensive. Once the secret for making hard-paste porcelain was discovered at Meissen in 1709, other European rulers pursued the recipe with a passion that is hard for us to imagine today.[22] In 1718 Peter negotiated to bring Peter Eggebrecht, a Dutch porcelain specialist then living in Dresden, to his capital city, but these arrangements ultimately fell through.[23] Russia would not have its own porcelain factory until after Peter's daughter Elizabeth came to the throne more than twenty years later.

During the reigns of the empresses Elizabeth (r. 1741–1761) and Catherine the Great (r. 1762–1796), Peter's dreams were solidified or realized. The rococo face of St. Petersburg resulted from the numerous commissions Elizabeth gave her favorite architect, Bartolomeo Rastrelli. She founded the Imperial Porcelain Factory in 1744 and the Academy of Arts in 1758. She modernized the primitive Imperial Lapidary Works at Peterhof in 1748 and established a polishing mill at Ekaterinburg in the Urals in 1755.[24]

Catherine's accomplishments in promoting the arts have been well documented. She was so enamored of building that she likened it to an illness.[25] This passion was exceeded only by that of collecting. She was a serious patron of all the court industries, particularly the Imperial Porcelain Factory and the Imperial Glassworks, which came under court control in 1791. Catherine also encouraged the exploration for minerals and initiated efforts to set up another lapidary factory at Kolyvan in the Altai Mountains.

Like their fellow autocrats in western Europe, the Russian monarchs of the eighteenth century were the chief arbiters of fashionable taste. The wealthiest members of the aristocracy eagerly followed their ruler's lead. In stark contrast, however, the urban middle class that was rapidly growing in France under Louis XV and Louis XVI was nowhere to be found in Russia at that time.

The diffusion of wealth into other classes began to take place in the first half of the nineteenth century and then only slowly. Both Alexander I (r. 1801–1825) and his brother Nicholas I (r. 1825–1855) continued to support cultural institutions in the eighteenth-century manner. In fact, Nicholas I rivaled

---

22. For more on the role of porcelain, see Anne Odom, "The Politics of Porcelain," in *At the Tsar's Table, Russian Imperial Porcelain from the Raymond F. Piper Collection* (Milwaukee, Wis.: Patrick and Beatrice Haggerty Museum of Art, 2001), 11–21.

23. [Baron Nikolai fon Vol'f], *Imperatorskii farforovyi zavod* (St. Petersburg: Izdanie Upravleniia imperatorskimi zavodami, 1906), Addendum, 3.

24. On lapidary works, see A.E. Fersman, *Ocherki po istorii kamnia*, vol. 2 (Moscow: Akademiia Nauk SSSR, 1961), 124–64.

25. Catherine wrote, "Building is a devilish affair. It eats money and the more one builds, the more one wants to build; it's an illness like drunkenness." Catherine to Baron Melchior von Grimm, in a letter dated 30 July 1779, in "Pis'ma Ekateriny Vtoroi k baronu Grimmu," *Russkii arkhiv*, vol. 3 (1878), 60.

his grandmother Catherine as a builder and as a patron of the arts. Alexander II (r. 1855–1881) did not share his father's passion for the arts. Beginning with the emancipation of the serfs in 1861, his extensive reforms, including legal, education, and local government measures, cleared the way for rapid industrial development. By the end of the nineteenth century the newly powerful merchants and industrialists started to play a more important role, both economically and as patrons.

THE REIGN OF NICHOLAS II

Luxury Industries during the Reign of Nicholas

Under Nicholas II (r. 1894–1917), the court continued to patronize most of those arts industries that Peter had sponsored or envisioned. What, however, had happened to them in the time since they were founded some two hundred years earlier? A turning point for the luxury industries was the Crimean War (1853–1855). Although these industries continued to play their traditional roles, the financial crises that followed Russian losses in the war led Alexander II to order severe cutbacks in production. For example, he closed the Imperial Tapestry Factory in 1859, considering it to be neither relevant nor affordable. The three lapidary factories remained in existence, but their artistic production was greatly diminished.[26] The Imperial Porcelain Factory also struggled financially.[27] At the same time that the porcelain industries were being revitalized in other parts of Europe, the Cabinet, which oversaw the court industries, believed the factory was a luxury and refused to modernize the physical plant. As a consequence, more effort was invested in making additions to old services than in creating new works.

The Imperial Porcelain Factory was incapable of producing a new porcelain service for use at the coronation of either Alexander III in 1883 or Nicholas II in 1896.[28] Even at the end of the nineteenth century Russia was

26. They were still participating in international expositions in 1893, and their products were greatly admired in the West. See *World's Columbian Exposition 1893. Catalogue of the Russian Section* (St. Petersburg: Ministry of Finances, Imperial Russian Commission, 1893), 189 and 191. The entry notes their "articles are either for the decoration of the palaces, or are given away as presents by order of His Majesty the Emperor."

27. For more in English about the Imperial Porcelain Factory, see Anne Odom, *Russian Imperial Porcelain at Hillwood* (Washington, D.C.: Hillwood Museum and Gardens, 1999).

28. The factory turned to the Factory of the Brothers Kornilov for help in producing additional white ware, but it was refused. The problem was solved in one case by using flawed white ware and in the second case by reducing the size of the order. RGIA (Rossiiskii gosudarstvennyi istoricheskii arkhiv), *fond* 503, *opis* 1/471/1987, *delo* 217, 1882, and *fond* 503, *opis* 1/478/2014, *delo* 92, 1895.

still forced to look abroad to find not only highly trained technicians but also skilled artists. Alexander III (r. 1881–1894), for example, invited Danish artists to St. Petersburg to teach his artisans the ancient Chinese technique of underglaze painting after the Royal Porcelain Factory of Copenhagen created a sensation with its display of wares employing this newly revived technique at the Exposition Universelle in Paris in 1889.

International expositions, beginning with the Great Exhibition of the Works of Industry of All Nations at the Crystal Palace in London in 1851, played an extremely important role as the nineteenth-century equivalent, at least in part, of the impressive court ceremonies of the previous century. Each nation competed at these venues to show off its latest advances in productivity and artistic ingenuity. All arts industries were under considerable scrutiny as art experts and critics in attendance compared the works on display and communicated their views via the press to the broader public.

At an international ceramics and glass exhibition held in St. Petersburg in 1901, Russians themselves had a chance to assess the production of their factories as well as that of the leading foreign factories. The comparison was hardly favorable. The critic for the prominent art journal *Mir iskusstva* (World of Art) praised the high technical quality of the Imperial Factory but severely criticized it for being content with "slavish imitation," insisting that it should "move forward, create new forms, and discover a new way."[29] Excited by the Western display, S.M. Kornilov wrote in *Iskusstvo i khudozhestvennaia promyshlennost'* (Art and Industry) that the Russian section of the exhibition was of little interest "due to the absence of artistic independence."[30] The Imperial Glassworks suffered from both financial and organizational problems and also received criticism at the 1901 exhibition, where it was unfavorably compared to Tiffany and Daum.[31]

In the field of art, both Alexander III and Nicholas II are most widely known for their patronage of the firm of Fabergé. Since Peter's day the leading silversmiths, with a few exceptions, were foreigners who had come to Russia, especially to St. Petersburg, to work for the court. Gustav Fabergé was just one of those foreigners and was succeeded by his son, Peter Carl, in

29. D. Bezhantskii, "Vystavka keramicheskikh izdelii," *Mir iskusstva* 1 (1901), 51.

30. S.M. Kornilov, "Po povodu Mezhdunarodnoi Keramicheskoi vystavki v Peterburge," *Iskusstvo i khudozhestvennaia promyshlennost'* 1 (January 1901), xxxix–xl.

31. Bezhantskii, 52. In 1881 the Ministry of the Imperial Court, which oversaw its operation, suggested that it be transferred to the Academy of Arts. This advice was ignored, and in 1900 the Imperial Glassworks was closed. A skeleton staff was merged with that of the Imperial Porcelain Factory. For more on the Imperial Glassworks, see Karen L. Kettering, *Russian Glass at Hillwood* (Washington, D.C.: Hillwood Museum and Gardens, 2001).

1872.[32] After years spent repairing the crown jewels, Carl Fabergé received the Imperial Warrant in 1885, distinguishing him as a supplier to the court. In that same year Alexander III commissioned Fabergé to fashion an egg to present to his wife Maria Fedorovna at Easter. Thus began the extraordinary annual commissions that culminated in the Fabergé firm's production of fifty-two imperial Easter eggs.[33]

By the time of the 1900 Exposition Universelle in Paris, Fabergé had achieved considerable fame. He exhibited there *hors concours* as a member of the jury. For his display at the exposition he was granted permission to fabricate a replica of the crown jewels, and Empress Alexandra generously allowed him to exhibit some of the imperial Easter eggs. This was the first time anyone outside the imperial family had seen these extraordinary creations. His French hosts honored Fabergé by awarding him the Cross of the Legion of Honor for his exceptional work.

Fabergé's production, considered technically remarkable, did not receive universal acclaim. His historicist styles looked somewhat old-fashioned to viewers in fin-de-siècle Paris. The showcase of his chief competitor, René Lalique, dazzled the critics. In spite of criticism from art nouveau enthusiasts, Fabergé emerged as the first jeweler in Russia to exert an influence on his Western peers, in particular the French jewelers Cartier and Boucheron.

In 1902 Empress Alexandra sponsored a charity exhibition of Fabergé's work in the von Derviz Palace on the English Embankment in St. Petersburg. This proved to be a unique opportunity for Russians to see many of the imperial Easter eggs for themselves. Members of the imperial family generously loaned objects to the exhibition.[34] While the St. Petersburg daily *Novoe vremia* was enthusiastic about the work presented, Alexander Benois, a leading figure in the World of Art community, wrote that Fabergé's work paled in comparison to the eighteenth-century masterpieces that were also on view.[35]

---

32. The amount of literature on Fabergé is enormous. See in particular Géza von Habsburg and Marina Lopato, *Fabergé: Imperial Jeweller* (Washington, D.C.: Fabergé Arts Foundation, 1993); Géza von Habsburg, *Fabergé* (Geneva: Habsburg, Feldman Editions, 1987); and Anne Odom, *Fabergé at Hillwood* (Washington, D.C.: Hillwood Museum and Gardens, 1998). For information about the imperial Easter eggs, see Tatiana Fabergé, Valentin Skurlov, and Lynette Proler, *Fabergé Easter Eggs* (London: Christie's, 1997).

33. After Alexander's death, Nicholas continued the tradition by giving one Easter egg to his wife and another one to his mother. No eggs were produced in 1904 and 1905, and the figure of fifty-two assumes that eggs were made in 1917, if not completed or delivered. See Fabergé, Skurlov, and Proler.

34. Marina Lopato, "New Insights into Fabergé from Russian Documents," in von Habsburg and Lopato, 65–66.

35. Lopato, 65, and Aleksandr Benua, "Khronika," *Mir iskusstva* 3 (1902), 66.

Even at home Fabergé was not without competitors. The St. Petersburg firms of Carl Bolin, Karl Hahn (Gan), and Ivan Britsyn all created works in the Fabergé style. In Moscow the production of two firms—Pavel Ovchinnikov and Ivan Khlebnikov—equaled that of Fabergé, but they worked primarily in the Russian style.[36] Ovchinnikov was the more experimental of the two, trying all the old native techniques and reviving ornament from the seventeenth century. They are most widely known for the thousands of small objects created for sale in their shops, but they received large commissions as well. Ovchinnikov and Khlebnikov both made grand liturgical sets for the consecration of the Cathedral of Our Savior in Moscow at the time of Alexander III's coronation in 1883. Ovchinnikov restored the iconostasis, or altar screen, of the Dormition Cathedral between 1881 and 1883 for the ceremony.[37] In 1894 the court commissioned the firm of Khlebnikov to devise a new enameled gilt-bronze iconostasis in the Annunciation Cathedral in the Kremlin, and for the 1913 Tercentenary celebrations the firm restored the tombs of the patriarchs in the Dormition Cathedral. That these projects were funded in large part by donations from Moscow's business elite reveals a significant shift in patronage.[38]

THE IMPERIAL FAMILY AS PATRONS

By the time Nicholas II (fig. 7) came to the throne in 1894, Russia had modernized dramatically. Alexander II's "great reforms" and the end of serfdom in 1861 left the nobility, especially those of the lesser ranks, impoverished. Many nobles became civil servants, but the more talented ones went into business. The country was undergoing industrialization at an intense pace, and these new merchants and industrialists were rapidly replacing the established nobility and the imperial court as tastemakers and community leaders. Their patronage stirred up a buzzing hive of artistic creativity in both Moscow and St. Petersburg.

---

36. Following their deaths, their firms were taken over by their sons. For more on the silversmiths who produced enamels, see Anne Odom, *Russian Enamels. From Kievan Rus to Fabergé* (London: Philip Wilson, 1996), 107–74. On Ovchinnikov see also Galina Smorodinova, "Pavel Ovchinnikov and Russian Gold- and Silversmithery," in *The Fabulous Epoch of Fabergé* (Moscow: Nord Publishers, 1992), 57–60, and on Khlebnikov see S.Ia. Kovarskaia, *Proizvedeniia moskovskoi iuvelirnoi firmy Khlebnikova* (Moscow: Moscow Kremlin, 2001).

37. *Vsemirnaia illiustratsiia* 30 (1883), 428–29, and Kovarskaia 2001, 10–11.

38. Kovarskaia 2001, 17, 20–24, 32–57, and Svetlana Kovarskaia, "... Ne meniat staryi oklad," *Mir muzeia* 2/174 (March-April 2000), 40–44.

Fig. 7. Portrait of Nicholas II
Mikhail V. Rundaltsov, 1912. Pastel on paper
Hillwood Museum and Gardens (cat. 5)

While they were no longer the chief arbiters of fashionable taste, Nicholas and Alexandra and other members of the imperial family nevertheless played their part as patrons of numerous projects involving the arts, often through informal channels. Regrettably, scholars have overlooked their role for various ideological reasons.[39] Nicholas was not the collector of fine art that his father had been, but he nevertheless oversaw the opening of the Imperial Alexander III Museum, now the State Russian Museum, with his father's collection of Russian realist paintings as its core. Like his father, he patronized Fabergé as well as other prominent silversmiths and jewelers. He commissioned services from the Imperial Porcelain Factory and, like his predecessors, considered porcelain an appropriate imperial gift.

Nicholas was a ballet enthusiast, as his well-known liaison with the ballerina Mathilda Kshessinskaia before his marriage suggests. He was also knowledgeable about the theater, often attending performances in his youth. In the last years before World War I, he frequently took his two oldest daughters with him. He supported Diagilev's journal Mir iskusstva (World of Art) and regularly attended openings of exhibitions organized by him. At one opening he purchased a painting by Alexander Benois, and at another he bought works by Tiffany and the Abramtsevo workshops.[40] In 1900 he commissioned Valentin Serov, then recognized as one of the foremost artists in Russia, to paint two portraits of him: one was a formal parade portrait, while the other, the now-famous informal portrait, was presented to his wife as a gift.[41]

Grand Duke Georgii Mikhailovich (see fig. 5) and his wife Maria Georgievna (see fig. 4) play an important role in this discussion because their objects comprise the Middlebury collection. Georgii was one of the "Mikhailovichi," the sons of Mikhail Nikolaevich, the youngest son of Nicholas I. Thus Georgii was a first cousin once removed from Nicholas II. Like the rest of the male Romanovs, Georgii was brought up in the strict regimen that would prepare

---

39. The reason for their neglect by Soviet historians is obvious. Since 1991 this neglect is slowly being rectified. Most Western historians have relied on accounts of the intelligentsia, such as Alexander Benois, who were constantly displeased with reactions of members of the court but rarely mentioned them when they were helpful. This area requires significantly more study to ascertain the importance of their contributions. What follows here is a highly superficial account of their activities.

40. David Elliot, "Ruined Palaces," in The Twilight of the Tsars: Russian Art at the Turn of the Century (London: South Bank Center, 1991), 22. The Abramtsevo workshops outside Moscow produced objects in the Russian arts and crafts style.

41. See Elizabeth Kridl Valkenier, Valentin Serov. Portraits of Russia's Silver Age (Evanston, Ill.: Northwestern University Press, 2001), 127–28, for a description of these sittings. The original informal portrait was destroyed during the Revolution; a copy is now in the Tretiakov Gallery in Moscow.

him for the army, and he was enlisted in a regiment at an early age. It was considered unthinkable that any of the Romanov men might have other interests. Aleksandr Mikhailovich wrote, "My brother George [as a young boy] once chanced to confess his inclination for portrait painting. He was greeted with the ominous silence of all parties assembled at the table, and understood his mistake immediately afterward, when the majestic tower of cherry and vanilla ice-cream glided past his place without a stop."[42] Due to a leg injury he was unable to continue a military career, and in 1895 he became the director of the newly created Imperial Alexander III Museum. Georgii was a frequent visitor to Diagilev's exhibitions and regularly bought paintings and sculpture for the museum. He also collected Russian coins and medals, assembling before the Revolution the most extensive collection in Russia.[43] In 1904 Georgii Mikhailovich became the patron of the newly formed Russian Art and Industry Society in St. Petersburg, which lasted until 1917.[44]

His wife, Maria Georgievna, was the daughter of King George I of Greece, a brother of Dowager Empress Maria Fedorovna. Her mother, Olga Konstantinovna, was a sister of Grand Duke Konstantin Konstantinovich, so her connections with Russia predated her marriage to Georgii in 1900. The couple lived and entertained at the New Mikhailovskii Palace owned by Georgii's father, where Georgii's bachelor brother Sergei Mikhailovich "organized a full orchestra of amateur players and also a male choir in which he sang himself with his fine bass voice."[45] The famed opera singer Fedor Chaliapin was invited to sing there in the presence of the emperor and empress. Maria's love of music was acknowledged around 1911 when Elizaveta Fedorovna, sister of the empress and wife of Grand Duke Sergei Aleksandrovich, asked Maria to replace her as president of the Philharmonic Society in Moscow.[46]

In a possible trial separation from her husband, Maria Georgievna left Russia in 1914 with her two daughters on a visit to England, where she was

---

42. Alexander, Grand Duke of Russia, 18.

43. Georgii gave his collection, about which he wrote several volumes, to the Alexander III Museum in 1909. About thirteen thousand pieces of this collection are now in the National Museum of American History, Smithsonian Institution, in Washington, D.C. At the time of the Revolution, four crates made their way out of Russia and came into the hands of Georgii's wife. See http://americanhistory.si.edu/csr/nnc/russianc/mikh.htm.

44. D.Ia. Severiukhin and O.L. Leikind, Zolotoi vek khudozhestvennykh ob"edinenii v Rossii i SSSR (1820–1932), (St. Petersburg: Tip. Chernysheva, 1992), 254. Established by teachers and graduates of the Central School of Technical Drawing, which had been founded by Baron Stieglitz, the society included artists who provided designs for Fabergé and the Kornilov Porcelain Factory.

45. A Romanov Diary, 101.

46. A Romanov Diary, 147. After Grand Duke Sergei was assassinated in 1905, Elizaveta became a nun.

stranded for the duration of the war.[47] Although Georgii Mikhailovich managed to smuggle letters through to his exiled family even after he was arrested, he never saw his wife and daughters again and was shot to death by the Bolsheviks in 1919.

Other grand dukes were active in the cultural world of St. Petersburg. Georgii's oldest brother, Nikolai Mikhailovich, was a serious historian;[48] Grand Duke Konstantin Konstantinovich, a cousin of Alexander III, was esteemed as president of the Academy of Sciences and a poet; Vladimir Aleksandrovich, one of Nicholas's uncles, was president of the Academy of Arts from 1880 until his death in 1909.[49] Pëtr Nikolaevich, a cousin of Georgii Mikhailovich, was an amateur architect who created several designs for religious objects.[50] As the emperor's brother, Mikhail Aleksandrovich, honorary chairman of the St. Petersburg Photographic Society, was in a position to arrange a meeting between Nicholas and the now-famous photographer Sergei Prokudin-Gorskii, which resulted in the photographer receiving permission to travel all over Russia from 1909 to 1915 to produce color photographs of the vast empire.[51] For artists, many of these contacts with members of the imperial family proved to be invaluable in the advancement of their careers.

Most major cultural institutions—the Academy of Arts, the Imperial Theaters, and the Conservatories, to name only a few—were still financed and managed by the court. Instruction in these institutions may have seemed restrictive to contemporaries, but many of the artistic giants of the early twentieth century, including composer Sergei Prokofiev, dancer Vaslav Nijinsky, and choreographer George Balanchine, received their training or taught in one of these institutions.[52]

With certain exceptions the tastes of the court were conservative; the imperial family and aristocrats favored Western classical and rococo styles. For both ceremonial and personal use, members of the court and the imperial

---

47. A grandson, David Chavchavadze, suggests that Maria might have planned a separation. See David Chavchavadze, *The Grand Dukes* (New York: Atlantic Publications, 1990), 185.

48. He wrote a biography of Alexander I and produced the four-volume work on Russian historical biography that is still widely used today.

49. Grand Duke Vladimir was passionate about the arts. He collected icons and contemporary porcelain vases from the Imperial Porcelain Factory, some of which are still in the Vladimir Palace today.

50. See *Svetil'nik* 1 (1913), plate opposite page 20, and 3 (1913), plate opposite page 18, for two examples.

51. Robert H. Allhouse, ed., *Photographs for the Tsar. The Pioneering Photography of Sergei Mikhailovich Prokudin-Gorskii Commissioned by Nicholas II* (New York: Dial Press, 1980), xiv–xviii.

52. John O. Norman emphasizes this point in his chapter "Alexander III as Patron of Russian Art," in *New Perspectives on Russian and Soviet Artistic Culture*, ed. by John O. Norman (New York: St. Martin's Press, 1994), 34–35.

family tended to patronize the imperial factories and the firm of Fabergé. As we shall see, however, they often preferred native Russian styles when commissioning objects as gifts for foreigners or when ordering designs for new church buildings and their furnishings. In contrast, the new industrialists, bankers, and urban middle class were much more eclectic in their tastes, often patronizing the production of the private factories, the arts and crafts communities at the country estates of Abramtsevo and Talashkino, the art schools, and independent artists.

CEREMONY AT THE RUSSIAN COURT

Coronation

Nicholas, Alexandra, and other members of the court turned again and again to their traditional suppliers for presentation gifts and to enhance court life in the last decades of the empire. Despite the Western styles produced by the Imperial Porcelain Factory and the firm of Fabergé in particular, pre-Petrine symbolism and references to seventeenth-century Russia pervade many court ceremonies. That they should be employed at the time of the tercentenary of Romanov rule in 1913 is not surprising, but they appear already at the coronation of Nicholas II in 1896. The public messages this imagery implied were in complete contrast to the daily life that the imperial family actually led.

Official ceremonies held during the reign of Nicholas II remained the principal vehicle for "the theater of self-presentation." None was more important than the crowning of Nicholas II as emperor in the Dormition Cathedral of the Moscow Kremlin in May 1896. If one purpose of the coronation was to reveal the magnificence of the Russian court to guests from all over the Western world, the Russians did not disappoint them. At least one foreign visitor viewed the celebration as "Versailles relived," thus projecting eighteenth-century absolutism into the late nineteenth century.[53] Certainly, given Nicholas's view of himself as the "Autocrat of All the Russias," this was an accurate perception. Riches were seen everywhere; visitors could not help but be awed by the lavish display of sparkling jewels and elaborate dress. The number of people present not only greatly exceeded those who attended the coronation of his father, Alexander III, but also included far more press, both Russian and foreign, ensuring that word of the grandeur of the Russian court would be disseminated worldwide.[54]

---

53. Quoted in Wortman, 2: 349.
54. Wortman, 2: 345.

At the same time, the Orthodox service in the Dormition Cathedral, where tsars had been crowned since time immemorial, the specially made vestments of the clergy fashioned after a seventeenth-century prototype (cat. 11),[55] the design of the announcement (cat. 9), the extensive menu (fig. 8), and the coronation albums (cat. 14), which all linked Nicholas to his august pre-Petrine Romanov ancestors, reminded guests that this was Moscow and not Versailles. Underscoring the tone, the menu that Viktor Vasnetsov designed for the coronation banquet held in the fifteenth-century Faceted Hall of the Kremlin recalled the coronation of the first Romanov in 1613 (see fig. 1). At the top of the menu, in a reserve in the shape of a three-domed church, the young Michael Romanov (r. 1613–1645) is being crowned by the boyars. This image is a detail taken from a seventeenth-century manuscript that had been reprinted in 1856, probably for the coronation of Alexander II.[56] Below the inscription the boyars greet the new tsar with bread and salt, the traditional ceremony of welcome. At the bottom are peacocks, a Byzantine symbol of immortality; a pair of them often decorated early Russian manuscripts.

Banquets, opera performances, troop reviews, and presentations by delegations representing the great diversity of the Russian empire were part of the two-week festivities. One day was devoted to Nicholas receiving greetings from representatives of towns, provinces, and societies, who in turn presented the emperor with bread and salt (fig. 9).[57] Icons and other objects that represented the traditional manufacture of a specific region, however, were also deemed appropriate.

---

55. The vestments were designed after one made for Patriarch Adrian two hundred years earlier in 1696. See *Sobranie pamiatnikov tserkovnoi stariny* (Moscow: Izdanie tserkovnoi iubileinoi komissii, 1913), 79–80.

56. For the image on the menu, see *Rossiiskii gerb 500 let. Iubileinaia vystavka* (Moscow, 1997), 12. For an example of this event depicted on an enamel plaque made at the Imperial Stroganov School, see Odom 1986, 156 bottom. These images were taken from a book about the election of Tsar Mikhail called *Kniga ob izbranii na prevysochaishii prestol' velikago Rossiiskago tsarstviia Velikago Gosudaria, Tsaria i Velikago kniazia Mikhaila Feodorovicha, vseia Rossii Samoderzhtsa.* See A. Mironoff, "O podlinnykh i nedostovernykh portretakh tsaria Mikhaila Feodorovicha (XVII–XVIII stoletii)," *Starye gody* (July-September 1913), plate opposite page 11 and pages 11–12. The image is outlined in a white floral pattern on black, which was derived from a sixteenth-century ornament illustrated in the design book by Vladimir Butovskii, *Histoire de l'ornement russe du Xe au XVIe siècle d'après les manuscrits* (Paris: Vve A. Morel cie, 1870), pls. XX, XXI, and XCIV.

57. At the time of his coronation Nicholas received 285 silver bread and salt dishes. See *Koronatsionyi sbornik*, vol. 1 (1899), 293. One hundred twenty are illustrated in *Tsarskie koronatsii na Rusi. Iz istorii derzhavy rossiiskoi XVI–XX vv* (New York: Russian Orthodox Youth Committee, 1971). Grand Duke Konstantin Konstantinovich complained in his diary about these presents: "A constant stream of costly dishes were offered with bread and salt; . . . what a useless expense! How much good could that amount of money have been put to!" Andrei Maylunas and Sergei Mironenko, *A Lifelong Passion. Nicholas and Alexandra, Their Own Story* (New York: Doubleday, 1997), 144.

Fig. 8. Coronation menu, 1896
Colored lithograph after a drawing by Viktor Vasnetsov
Hillwood Museum and Gardens (cat. 10)

Fig. 9. Bread and salt ceremony held in the Kremlin Palace
at the coronation of Nicholas II. *Niva,* 1896

One bread and salt dish has as its central decoration the intertwined ciphers of Nicholas II and Alexandra topped by the imperial double-headed eagle (fig. 10). The personal coat of arms of the emperor appears at the top of this dish.[58] At the bottom are Saint George and the dragon, the coat of arms of Moscow, and the crossed anchors of St. Petersburg in *kokoshnik*-shaped reserves. Flowers outlined in gold, of a type found on late seventeenth-century enamels made in the Russian north, surround the cipher and coats of arms. The dish, like most of the silver ones presented at the coronation, is decorated in the Russian style, but it also represents the creative work of a growing number of artists who were not attached to one of the leading factories.

Whether this particular bread and salt dish was presented at the time of the coronation is unclear; it might have been given at any of numerous other

58. For the coat of arms, see Petr Grebel'skii and Aleksandr Mirvis, *Dom Romanovykh. Biograficheskie svedeniia o chlenakh tsarstvovavshego doma, ikh predkakh i rodstvennikakh* (St. Petersburg: LIO Redaktor, 1992), 238. The personal coat of arms of the emperor consisted of two parts: the Romanov family griffin on the left and the shield of Holstein-Gottorp on the right. The Holstein-Gottorp shield was probably added in 1761 when Karl Peter Ulrich, the head of the house of Holstein-Gottorp, became emperor as Peter III. Peter was the nephew of Elizabeth I and husband of the future Catherine II.

Fig. 10. Bread and salt dish, 1894–96. A. Glazunova, painter. Faience
Hillwood Museum and Gardens (cat. 12)

events held between Nicholas's marriage in 1894 and his coronation in 1896.[59] One such occasion occurred shortly after the couple's marriage, when Alexandra was introduced to the court on New Year's Day 1895. On this occasion the young couple was showered with hundreds of gifts.[60]

The Tercentenary

The three hundredth anniversary of Romanov rule in 1913 offered another major occasion for ceremonies throughout the country, and another opportunity for Nicholas to unite himself with his forefathers, especially the first Romanov, Tsar Michael.

Ceremonies for the Tercentenary took place in St. Petersburg, in Moscow, and in Kostroma on the Volga, the historic seat of the Romanovs. Nicholas made every effort at these ceremonies to link himself to Tsar Michael, who had brought peace and stability to Russia after the disturbances of the Time of Troubles.[61] Referring to Michael served as a reminder that Russia could not allow autocratic power to be weakened. For Alexander III and his son, Nicholas II, it was not the reign of Peter the Great and the founding of St. Petersburg in 1703 that marked the beginning of modern Russian history, but rather the accession to the throne of Tsar Michael.[62]

The Cap of Monomakh, the traditional crown of pre-Petrine Russia, came to be regarded as one of the central symbols of the Tercentenary. It appeared in graphic designs—Tsar Michael wears it on the menu for the Tercentenary banquet (cat. 22)—and was seen on numerous souvenirs of the occasion, such as a miniature pendant that features the Cap of Monomakh with three tiny carnelian drops (cat. 16). The emperor commissioned special brooches to be presented to the ladies of the court at this time. Empress Alexandra herself sent to Fabergé the original drawings she had prepared for them. These commemorative gifts, as finally realized by Fabergé, came in varying designs (fig. 11).[63]

---

59. The luxury volume (cat. 14) that was published to commemorate the coronation mentions one faience plate from the Village Society of Chumiakovskii district in the Cheliabinsk region. See *Koronatsionnyi sbornik*, vol. 2 (1899), 222. The plate is signed by a woman, O. Glazunova, about whom nothing is known. The mark is not known either, but it is probably that of a foreign faience factory. Importing finished white ware for painting was not a new practice in Russia.

60. Buxhoeveden, 53–54.

61. The last of the Riurik tsars, Tsar Fedor, son of Ivan the Terrible, died in 1598. The period between his death and the election of Michael Romanov in 1613 is known as the Time of Troubles due to the inner strife, foreign intervention, and anarchy that plagued the land.

62. Wortman, 2: 440.

63. Henry Charles Bainbridge, *Peter Carl Fabergé. Goldsmith and Jeweller to the Russian Court* (London: Spring Books, 1949), 56. For another style of brooch, see von Habsburg and Lopato, 262–63.

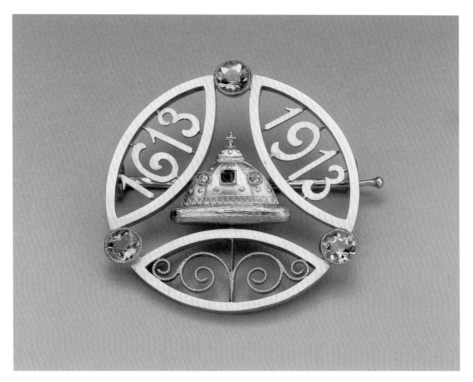

Fig. 11. Tercentenary brooch, 1913. Firm of Fabergé, Albert Holmström, workmaster
Gold, aquamarine, rubies, diamonds. Hillwood Museum and Gardens (cat. 17)

Princess Cantacuzene, the granddaughter of President Ulysses S. Grant and the wife of a Russian prince, remembered that in 1913 "an official reception occurred at the Winter Palace, when each guest in national Costume was given a golden insignia to mark his or her attendance at Court."[64] These brooches continued to be distributed throughout the course of 1913, and some were even presented in 1914. The Hillwood brooch, one of two hundred made, was awarded on 2 July 1914 to Maria Vedrinskaia, an actress associated with the imperial theaters.[65]

References to old Russia were everywhere. At the banquet held at the Kremlin on 25 May 1913, the table was set with the Kremlin Service that Nicholas I had commissioned in 1837 (fig. 12). Its designer, Fedor Solntsev, utilized several Old Russian motifs. The ornament of the dessert plate, for example, derived from a gold and enamel plate that had been made in the

---

64. Princess Cantacuzene, Countess Speransky, née Grant, *My Life Here and There* (New York: Charles Scribner's Sons, 1921), 314–15.

65. RGIA, *fond* 468, *opis* 8, *delo* 1290, *list* 3–4. I wish to thank Valentin Skurlov for this information.

Kremlin Armory workshops in 1667 for Tsar Aleksei, Peter's father.[66] Intended for five hundred people, the service included two thousand dinner plates, one thousand soup plates, and one thousand dessert plates.[67] For the rest of the nineteenth century it was used for coronations, and by the time of the Tercentenary it was known as the "rich [bogatyi] Moscow service." Nicholas ordered additions to the service from the Imperial Factory for the Tercentenary.[68] At the same time he also commissioned a large number of glasses to be used with the Kremlin Service (see page 84).[69]

Nicholas II used Old Russian ornament to reinforce his position as autocrat of all the Russias, just as Catherine the Great had employed classical imagery to support her claim to legitimacy. Both the Cap of Monomakh and the Kremlin Service strengthened his dynastic connection to the early Romanovs by invoking Russia's wealth of native visual culture before Westernization had completely replaced it.

Official Presentations

Russians were always particularly lavish with the presentation of gifts, publicly and privately. Russian enamels made by the Moscow firms of Pavel Ovchinnikov and Ivan Khlebnikov rivaled the works of Fabergé as appropriate official presents, particularly those given to foreign delegations. Nicholas I opened the door to new ornament possibilities that reflected Russia's native heritage when he funded the publication of Solntsev's drawings of the antiquities in the Kremlin Armory. Published in the 1850s, they inspired numerous books on Russian ornament that came to serve as sources for future designers working in the decorative arts.[70] The resulting Russian style flourished in the late nineteenth century in the hands of Fabergé's principal competitors in Moscow. Bread and salt dishes in the Russian style were especially popular gifts at the coronations of both Alexander III and Nicholas II.

In the 1890s the firm of Ovchinnikov made many tankards that were frequently presented as gifts to visiting delegations. Ovchinnikov employed as

---

66. For the origins of the Kremlin Service, see Anne Odom, "Fedor Solntsev, the Kremlin Service, and the Origins of the Russian Style," *The Post*, Hillwood Studies (fall 1991), 1–4.

67. RGIA, *fond* 468, *opis* 10, *delo* 821, 1837, *list* 18.

68. RGIA, *fond* 503, *opis* 2, *delo* 483, *list* 21 and 23. I wish to thank Tamara Kudriavtseva for providing the information in this note and the next one.

69. RGIA, *fond* 468, *opis* 26, *delo* 256, *list* 85 ob. These were apparently additions to an existing set.

70. Solntsev's work was produced in six volumes as *Drevnosti rossiiskago gosudarstva* (St. Petersburg: Imperial Archeological Commission, 1846–1853).

Fig. 12. Dessert plate from the Kremlin Service, 1837–55
Imperial Porcelain Factory, Fedor Solntsev, designer. Hard-paste porcelain
Hillwood Museum and Gardens (cat. 20)

a prototype an example that Solntsev had defined as "Eastern" and included in his drawings of works in the Kremlin Armory. He thus turned an object of Eastern origin, that is, either Turkish or Persian, into a quintessentially Russian type (fig. 13).[71] This particular tankard is identical in form to one the city officials of St. Petersburg presented to visiting French officers in 1897.[72]

Porcelain vases had been a favorite imperial gift dating from the time of Nicholas I. According to family oral history, Nicholas II presented a splendid vase (fig. 14), made at the Imperial Porcelain Factory in 1907, to the mayor of Vologda in remembrance of his visit to the Church of Serafim of Sarov, where he gave thanks for the birth of Tsarevich Aleksei in 1904. As we have seen, anything connected with Serafim of Sarov held special significance for the emperor. The white ground of the vase is decorated with simple raised green vines that climb to the top where they intertwine. Its graceful but simple art nouveau style exemplifies the best work of the Imperial Factory in a period when its production was, on the whole, in decline.

A defining event in the reign of Nicholas II was the Russo-Japanese War of 1904–1905, in which the Japanese completely destroyed Russia's Far Eastern fleet. This defeat humiliated Russia's leadership, which was at the same time badly shaken by riots in the streets and uprisings in the countryside. American president Theodore Roosevelt brokered the peace settlement signed in Portsmouth, New Hampshire, on 5 September 1905 (N.S.). A small enameled dish or ashtray by Fabergé (fig. 15) inscribed to "CN" was probably presented to Konstantin Nabokov (using the Latin spelling of his name, Constantine), who was secretary of the Russian delegation at the conference. Set with a coin dated 1772 from the time of Catherine, it is quite typical of many Fabergé ashtrays.[73] The great writer Vladimir Nabokov, Konstantin's nephew, recalled in his memoir *Speak, Memory* that "we drift past the show windows of Fabergé whose mineral monstrosities, jeweled troikas poised on marble ostrich eggs, and the like, highly appreciated by the imperial family, were emblems of grotesque garishness to ours."[74] We can imagine that his uncle, however,

---

71. See Odom 1996, 120–21, for another example and its prototype.

72. Odom 1996, 122, and *Vsemirnaia illiustratsiia*, 6 September [1897]. Georgii Aleksandrovich, Nicholas II's brother, gave one of the same shape to William F. "Buffalo Bill" Cody, probably in 1892, when Buffalo Bill was on a cruise of the Black Sea. See Butterfield advertisement in *Maine Antique Digest* (August 2000), 17-G.

73. See Marvin C. Ross, *The Art of Karl Fabergé and His Contemporaries* (Norman, Okla.: University of Oklahoma Press, 1965), 83–84, for more on Nabokov, and plates 21 and 22 for hardstone ashtrays set with coins.

74. Vladimir Nabokov, *Speak, Memory: An Autobiography Revisited* (New York: G.P. Putnam and Sons, 1966), 111.

Fig. 13. Tankard, 1890. Firm of Ovchinnikov
Silver gilt, enamel. Hillwood Museum and Gardens (cat. 23)

Fig. 14. Vase, 1907. Imperial Porcelain Factory. Hard-paste porcelain
On loan to Middlebury College Museum of Art (cat. 29)

Fig. 15. Presentation ashtray, ca. 1905
Firm of Fabergë, probably Anders Nevaleinen, workmaster. Silver gilt, enamel
Hillwood Museum and Gardens (cat. 27)

might have approved of this small Fabergé dish, which was far more tasteful than the items Vladimir described.

Nicholas and other members of the imperial family devoted considerable thought and expense to the numerous gifts they presented to those who had performed services or given pleasure. Ballerinas and actresses frequently received lavish imperial favors. In her memoirs the prima ballerina Mathilda Kshessinskaia describes gifts of jewels and objects made by Fabergé. Each Easter, Grand Duke Vladimir Aleksandrovich, the father of her future husband Andrei, gave her "an enormous egg-shaped bouquet of lilies of the valley with a precious stone, also in the shape of an egg."[75]

Nicholas himself presented gifts to various ballerinas and actresses. In 1901 he gave a diamond-studded pendant watch to the French actress Mademoiselle

---

75. The Princess H.S.H. Romanovsky-Krassinsky, *Dancing in Petersburg. The Memoirs of Kschessin-ska* (Garden City, N.Y.: Doubleday, 1961), 95.

Fig. 16. Pendant watch, ca. 1901. Gold, diamonds, enamel.
Hillwood Museum and Gardens (cat. 25)

Margarita Barety of the Imperial Mikhailovskii Theater (fig. 16).[76] The watch, decorated with a double-headed eagle, is suspended on a chain from a replica of the imperial crown, all covered with diamonds. Men's pocket watches, usually embellished with the double-headed eagle in enamel, were frequent gifts from the emperor. One of the clergy, the Archdeacon Popov, who officiated at Aleksei's baptism in 1904, received just such a watch (cat. 26). It is clear that appropriate court presentation gifts to Russians were neoclassical in style, while the Old Russian style was generally reserved for foreigners.

Court Life

Although ceremonial life was often imbued, for both political and emotional reasons, with references to the pre-Petrine past of the Romanovs, court life itself, in terms of fashion, interior design, and most forms of entertainment,

---

76. She performed at the Mikhailovskii Theater, also called the French Theater, from 1898 to the end of the 1904–1905 season. She probably received this award for a benefit performance held on 23 February. See L.A. Gel'merson, ed., *Ezhegodnik imperatorskikh teatrov. Sezon 1901–02* (St. Petersburg: Direktsiia imperatorskikh teatrov, 1902), 220. Elizaveta Balletta, also an actress at this theater, received a miniature statue of Peter the Great mounted on an emerald. Now in the Hillwood collection, this piece was one of several Fabergé gifts presented to Mme. Balletta. See Odom 1998, 14, 17, and von Habsburg 1987, 182.

was entirely Western. Except for religious services, nothing in the everyday life of Nicholas's family distinguished it from that of his western European counterparts. Foreigners noticed, as they had for two centuries, that Russians considered anything foreign to be superior to what was made in Russia. Most members of the imperial family and court traveled widely, bought French fashions, shopped in Paris and in Russia for expensive jewelry at the shops of Cartier and Boucheron as well as Fabergé, and were fluent in at least three languages.

Although Nicholas enjoyed balls and the social life of St. Petersburg far more than his father had, his wife Alexandra was never comfortable in society. Nicholas soon came to prefer a quiet life with his family, going hunting or taking long walks in the woods around the Alexander Palace, which became the family's permanent residence in 1904, or in the parks at Gatchina or Peterhof. British historian Dominic Lieven likened Nicholas to his cousin George V in that both "were at heart country gentlemen."[77] The royal collections of both men included fabulous works of art that were installed in major architectural monuments. Yet in their personal lives Nicholas II and George V preferred living in the Victorian manner in rooms crowded with knick-knacks, picture frames, and memorabilia (fig. 17).[78]

At the beginning of his reign, Nicholas commissioned two new porcelain services whose artistic references were well-grounded in eighteenth-century rococo. The Aleksandrinskii Turquoise Service of 1899, named after Alexandra, was designated for the Winter Palace. Four years later, in 1903, Nicholas ordered the Purple Service (fig. 18) for use at Tsarskoe Selo, probably in the Catherine Palace.

The Imperial Porcelain Factory announced a competition for designs for the Purple Service.[79] By the end of the nineteenth century the Stroganov Central School for Applied Art in Moscow, the silversmith firms of Pavel Ovchinnikov and Ivan Khlebnikov in Moscow, the Society for the Encouragement of the Arts, and the Stieglitz Central School for Technical Drawing in St. Petersburg were already sponsoring such competitions. On this occasion the Imperial Factory called for designs to be rendered in the style of Bartolomeo Rastrelli, the eighteenth-century architect of the Winter Palace. According to

---

77. Dominic Lieven, Nicholas II. Twilight of the Empire (New York: St. Martin's Press, 1993), 29.

78. Nicholas and Alexandra lived at the Alexander Palace in a suite of rooms designed in the art nouveau style by the architect Roman Meltser. Alexandra's brother, Grand Duke Ernst Ludwig of Hesse-Darmstadt, was the founder of the art colony at Mathildenhöhe outside Darmstadt, famous for the art nouveau, or Jugendstil, works produced there.

79. The name probably derives from en camaieu purpe, the color used at Vincennes-Sèvres in the early 1750s.

Fig. 17. Maple Drawing Room in the Alexander Palace. Postcard from the collection of
Stephen de Angelis. The drawing room was named after Maple and Company in London,
which supplied the furniture and fabrics.

the widely advertised instructions, "the designs should be simple but rich."[80]
The winning entries did not satisfy Alexandra, who apparently supervised the
choice herself, so Emil Kremer, the head of the art workshop at the factory,
had to rework them.[81] Based on Meissen shapes and a combination of Meissen and Sèvres designs, the finished pieces have alternating panels of tooled
gold and monochrome pink-purple and white landscapes. Putti frolic in the
center of the dessert plates with reticulated borders.

The Imperial Porcelain Factory and the Imperial Glassworks also turned out
porcelain and glass for the imperial yachts. Alexander III commissioned the
imperial yacht *Polar Star* and laid its keel in 1888; it was launched two years
later. Nikolai Nabokov, who was later to plan a suite of rooms for Nicholas
and Alexandra in the Winter Palace, designed the furnishings for the yacht.
No special porcelain was created for the *Polar Star*, but the Glassworks produced a set of glass tumblers in several different colors (fig. 19). These sturdy
glasses, suitable for use on board ship, were engraved with the imperial

---

80. RGIA, *fond* 503, *opis* 1/491/2128, *delo* 128, *list* 18.
81. Baron fon Vol'f, the director of the Imperial Factory at this time, complained that many of
the drawings submitted to these competitions were of little use because the artists did not work
with porcelain and had no idea what was feasible. See [fon Vol'f], 315.

Fig. 18. Dessert plate from the Purple Service, 1905
Imperial Porcelain Factory. Hard-paste porcelain
Hillwood Museum and Gardens (cat. 30)

double-headed eagle. The Dowager Empress Maria traveled annually on the *Polar Star* on her trips home to Denmark, and Nicholas and Alexandra used the yacht when they made their tour of Europe in 1896 before the completion of their favorite yacht, the *Standart*.[82]

All the members of the imperial family commissioned flatware (cat. 35) and tea sets at the time of their marriages. Grand Duke Aleksandr Mikhailovich, who married Nicholas's sister Kseniia, was overwhelmed when taken to see "the exhibition of the trousseau" that included "silver plate for ninety-six persons."[83] By the end of the nineteenth century the chief suppliers of silver for the court and the aristocracy were the Brothers Grachëv and Fabergé in St. Petersburg, and Sazikov, Ovchinnikov, and Khlebnikov in Moscow. All the Moscow silversmiths had shops in Petersburg, and Fabergé's main production of silver took place in his Moscow workshops, which were founded in 1887.

Both the tea set and the flatware that belonged to Georgii Mikhailovich were made in 1894 by the St. Petersburg firm of the Brothers Grachëv (fig. 20). (A long-time bachelor, the grand duke did not marry until 1900 at the age of thirty-seven.) All the pieces are decorated with his monogram. The tea set is in the neo-rococo style, which became especially popular after the treaty of alliance with France was signed in 1894.

While balls, dinners, and receptions in the grand manner were still held, many aspects of court life changed over the course of the nineteenth century. The domestic pastimes of the imperial family became increasingly intimate and private, as they lived in cozy rooms filled with souvenirs, picture frames, and other memorabilia. Photography had attained great popularity by then, and Nicholas and his family were enthusiastic amateur photographers. People no longer took snuff; they smoked cigarettes. In keeping with the changing times, Fabergé and other jewelers created a whole group of practical objects, such as picture frames, ashtrays, and desk sets, for the home and the study. The nobility shared the imperial family's love of an abundance of small objects in their surroundings, much like the cluttered interiors now associated with the Victorian era. Princess Cantacuzene, in describing a call she made on the Dowager Empress Maria Fedorovna, remarked that the tables

---

82. For more about the yacht, see A.L. Larionov, "Iz istorii imperatorskikh iakht," in *Russkie imperatorskie iakhty. Konets XVII–nachalo XX veka* (St. Petersburg: EGO, 1997), 23–26. For more about the glass, see the same volume for the article by V.V. Znamenov and T.N. Nosovich, "Servizy imperatorskikh iakht, XIX–nachala XX veka," 42–43.

83. Alexander, Grand Duke of Russia, 132. According to François Birbaum, Fabergé made the flatware for Grand Duchess Kseniia and the firm of Edward Bolin produced the jewelry. Birbaum says this was also the case for the dowry of Olga Aleksandrovna, Nicholas's youngest sister, and for Nicholas himself. See "Birbaum Memoirs," von Habsburg and Lopato, 453.

Fig. 19. Two tumblers from the service for the imperial yacht *Polar Star*, ca. 1888
Imperial Glassworks. Glass. On loan to Middlebury College Museum of Art (cat. 32)

Fig. 20. Tea set, 1894. Firm of the Brothers Grachëv. Silver, gilding, ivory
Middlebury College Museum of Art, Gift of Nancy and Edward Wynkoop (cats. 33 and 34)

placed by the chairs where they sat "seemed covered with bits of old silver, tiny animals carved in precious stones by Fabergé, or various enamels of his making, a small clock among other things such as anyone might have in a sitting room; and the Empress herself looked at home here."[84] In the gift-giving society of Russia, a small box, a picture frame, or a hardstone animal was the perfect present. Nicholas, for example, noted in his diary on his birthday on 2 May 1894 that he had received "two pairs of lovely buttons and a heavenly green 'frog' (Fabergé)." Grand Duke Konstantin Konstantinovich, Nicholas's uncle, wrote in his diary on 21 May 1898, "In the evening the Tsar and Tsarina sent me a delightful Fabergé thermometer as a present."[85]

The functional but beautiful Karelian birch desk set is a perfect example of the exquisite neoclassical design and brilliant combination of materials that were Fabergé's trademark (fig. 21). The translucent white enamel panels mounted in gilded silver and set against the warm honey-colored birch are striking. Fabergé turned out an amazing number of items for the desk, including paperweights, stamp moisteners, seals, letter openers, pens, and pen rests.

All of these items seem to be missing from Nicholas's desk at the Alexander Palace (fig. 22). Instead, an array of photographs covers all but a small area for writing. The Middlebury collection includes a number of framed photographs and miniatures that have come down through the family. The frame commemorating the tenth anniversary of the wedding of Grand Duke Georgii Mikhailovich and his wife Maria Georgievna features a copper-washed Roman numeral ten (fig. 23).[86] It supports miniatures on ivory of the grand duke and his daughters, Nina and Xenia.

Two other family frames by Fabergé (fig. 24 and cat. 55) stand out as excellent examples of the firm's magnificent workmanship and attention to detail. Both are decorated with translucent enamel, one in light blue and red enamel, the other in lavender. The metal under the enamel has been engine turned, or machine engraved, so the pattern of the engraving shows through the enamel, as seen in the moiré pattern of the lavender frame. On the triptych frame the red enamel was colored to simulate wood. Another Fabergé characteristic was the use of varicolored gold, which can be seen in the swags at the top of the frames. The process involved adding different minerals, such as silver, copper, or platinum, to the gold to vary the shades. The triptych frame holds miniatures on ivory of Maria Georgievna and her two daughters,

---

84. Princess Cantacuzene, 229.

85. Maylunas and Mironenko, 65 and 172.

86. For another example with Grand Duke Georgii's brother Grand Duke Mikhail and his family, see von Habsburg 1987, 244.

Fig. 21. Part of a desk set, 1908–17
Firm of Fabergé, Henrik Wigström, workmaster. Birch, silver gilt, enamel
Hillwood Museum and Gardens (cat. 38)

Fig. 22. Working study of Nicholas II at the Alexander Palace
Postcard from the collection of Stephen de Angelis

Nina and Xenia. Photographs of Georgii Mikhailovich, Maria Georgievna, their daughter Nina, and granddaughter Nancy Wynkoop are mounted in the diptych.

Two tiny frames by Fabergé, one star-shaped and one round (fig. 25), should be compared with two miniature frames by the firm of Cartier (fig. 26). Fabergé's enormous influence on Cartier is immediately obvious. Cartier began sending representatives to Russia in 1904 to build up and supply his Russian clientele. He imitated Fabergé's style in order to capture this wealthy Russian market.[87] The Fabergé frames contain photographs of Grand Duke Georgii and his daughter Xenia. The green Cartier frame holds a photograph of Nicholas's oldest daughter Olga, and the salmon frame displays a photo of Tatiana, his second daughter.

According to a family story, Georgii Mikhailovich or his brother Sergei commissioned Fabergé to make an obsidian tapir, a shy, nocturnal animal that inhabits Central and South America, as a gift for Grand Duchess Maria (fig. 27). Very nearsighted, Maria wore a pince-nez. One of her brothers-in-law,

---

87. Hans Nadelhofer, *Cartier. Jewelers Extraordinary* (New York: Harry N. Abrams, 1984), chapter 7.

Fig. 23. Tenth Anniversary frame, ca. 1910
Firm of Fabergé, Hjalmar Armfelt, workmaster. Coppered silver, miniatures on ivory
Middlebury College Museum of Art, Gift of Nancy and Edward Wynkoop (cat. 54)

Fig. 24. Diptych frame, ca. 1908
Firm of Fabergé, Viktor Aarne, workmaster. Gold, enamel, diamonds, ivory, photographs
On loan to Middlebury College Museum of Art (cat. 56)

Fig. 25. Two frames, ca. 1904. Firm of Fabergé
Gold, silver, enamel, ivory, pearls, photographs
On loan to Middlebury College Museum of Art (cats. 57 and 58)

probably Sergei, supposedly teased her by saying she looked like a tapir wearing a pince-nez. He or Georgii even asked Fabergé to add a pince-nez to the tapir's nose.[88] Known for his sense of humor, Fabergé would have appreciated this family joke. His firm was famous for its production of hardstone animals, the most well known group being the one that beginning in 1907 King Edward VII ordered for his wife, Queen Alexandra, the sister of Maria Fedorovna.[89] Fabergé employed agate and jasper to create realistic coloring; other stones—lapis lazuli, nephrite, and quartz—were carved to accentuate the innate beauty of the stone. While the animals belonging to Queen Alexandra were by far the most famous, it is clear from Princess Cantacuzene's description of Maria Fedorovna's sitting room that hardstone animals decorated the private spaces of many members of the elite. Several other firms, especially Cartier, produced small carved animals as well.

88. Grand Duchess Maria is pictured with her glasses in *A Romanov Diary*, 68.

89. This set included all the animals on the farm at Sandringham. See A. Kenneth Snowman, *Fabergé: Jeweler to Royalty* (Washington, D.C.: Smithsonian Institution, 1983) and the numerous entries throughout that book.

Fig. 26. Two frames, ca. 1910
Firm of Cartier. Gold, silver, enamel, ivory, photographs
Hillwood Museum and Gardens (cat. 62)

Two tiny hardstone figures in the Middlebury collection, a "Chinaman" and Tweedledum from *Alice Through the Looking Glass*, are unusual (fig. 28). According to Henry Charles Bainbridge, manager of Fabergé's London branch, Fabergé conceived the idea of creating figures from a mixture of hardstones in response to Grand Duke Nikolai Mikhailovich's request for a caricature of Queen Victoria. Fabergé thought this would not work if the figurine were carved out of a single stone, but it might be a success, he imagined, if she were fashioned out of different colored stones.[90] Fabergé never made many of these figures, but most of the ones he eventually created were larger than these two.[91] Like the animals, these would have made charming conversation pieces.

Jewelry and silver tableware have always been the "bread and butter" items of any jeweler. Among the most unusual types of jewelry created by the firm

90. Bainbridge, 111.

91. A combined figure of Tweedledum and Tweedledee is in the Thai Royal Collection. See Roy D.R. Betteley, "Fabergé in Thailand," in Alexander von Solodkoff, *Masterpieces from the House of Fabergé* (New York: Harry N. Abrams, 1984), 141. No other figure of a Chinaman is known.

Fig. 27. Tapir, ca. 1900
Firm of Fabergé. Obsidian, gold, rubies
Middlebury College Museum of Art, Gift of Nancy and Edward Wynkoop (cat. 46)

Fig. 28. Figure of a "Chinaman" and Tweedledum, ca. 1907–14
Firm of Fabergé. Mixed hardstones, including obsidian, bowenite, lapis lazuli, agate
On loan to Middlebury College Museum of Art (cats. 47 and 48)

Fig. 29. Ice pendant, ca. 1910
Firm of Fabergé, Albert Holmström,
workmaster, Alma Phil, designer
Rock crystal, diamonds, platinum
Middlebury College Museum of Art,
Gift of Nancy and Edward Wynkoop
(cat. 63)

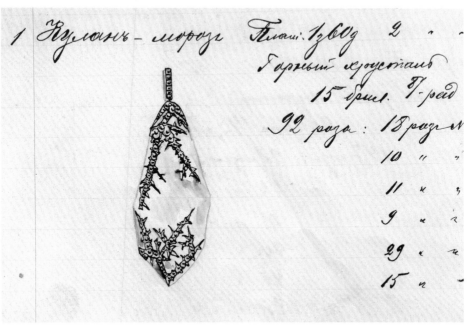

Fig. 30. Drawing of an ice pendant, ca. 1910
Alma Phil. Watercolor on paper. Courtesy Wartski's, London

were the so-called ice jewels. These were usually pendants made of rock crystal set with diamonds in designs made to look like frost crystallizations on a window (fig. 29). Alma Phil, the daughter of Knut Phil, one of Fabergé's workmasters, and Fanny Holmström, the daughter of August Holmström, a long-time Fabergé jeweler until his death in 1903, designed all these works. They were made in the workshops of Albert Holmström, Fanny's brother and Fabergé's chief jeweler.[92] One of Alma's designs is very similar to the Middlebury pendant (fig. 30).[93]

Emanuel Nobel, the Swedish oil magnate and one of Fabergé's foremost clients, ordered similar pendants. According to Bainbridge, "For Dr. Nobel a dinner party was no dinner at all unless the ladies present were suitably rewarded. On one of these occasions, wishing to recall a Russian winter, he conceived the idea of giving all the ladies present an icicle. Fabergé carried this out in pendants and brooches in rock-crystal with a matte surface adorned with small diamonds in frost design."[94]

Piety and Religious Faith

Despite their Westernized tastes and sense of style, Nicholas and Alexandra shared a religious faith that bordered on the mystical. Nicholas prayed daily, attended church regularly, and ensured that every official event included some form of prayer with clergy in attendance. His religious devotion is amply expressed in his diaries and letters, especially those he wrote to his mother.[95] When he and Alexandra went to Moscow for Easter in 1900, he wrote to his mother, "I never knew I was able to reach such religious ecstasy as this Lent has brought me to. The feeling is much stronger than it was in 1896, which is only natural. I am so calm and happy now, and everything here makes for prayer and peace of the spirit."[96] His relatives and advisers often remarked on Nicholas's calm in the face of major crises. This state of mind can be explained by his firm belief that whatever happened was God's will.

---

92. Holmström's workshop also produced small diamond-studded brooches in the shape of snowflakes. For several examples, including a bracelet, see von Habsburg and Lopato, 304–305.

93. For designs of other pendants, see von Habsburg 1987, 55. For a pendant in the Forbes Magazine Collection, see von Habsburg 1987, 143.

94. Bainbridge, 58.

95. See Maylunas and Mironenko throughout; Edward Bing, ed., *The Secret Letters of the Last Tsar. Being the Confidential Correspondence between Nicholas II and his Mother the Dowager Empress* (New York: Longmans, Green and Company, 1938). For a discussion of Nicholas's religious views, see Mark D. Steinberg, "Nicholas and Alexandra, an Intellectual Portrait," in *The Fall of the Romanovs. Political Dreams and Personal Struggles in a Time of Revolution*, ed. Mark D. Steinberg and Vladimir M. Khrustalëv (New Haven: Yale University Press, 1995), 12–14.

96. Bing, 137.

Fig. 31. Icon, Mother of God, "Surety of Sinners," early 20th century
Tempera on wood, gold, diamonds, emeralds, pearls, brass plaque
Hillwood Museum and Gardens (cat. 77)

This commitment to God led Nicholas and Alexandra to support various church projects. In 1902 and 1903 they took great interest in the building of the iconostasis that would stand in the church at Port Arthur, the new Russian naval base in Manchuria. They personally contributed three thousand rubles toward its construction. Their religious fervor coincided with a growing religious revival among many in Russian intellectual and artistic circles. As a result, Nicholas and the artists were often united by a common purpose. In 1901, for example, he approved the establishment of the Imperial Committee for the Preservation and Protection of Russian Icon Painting.[97] The committee's goal was to improve the sorry state into which traditional icon painting had fallen.

One of the most moving religious events for Nicholas was the 1903 glorification, or canonization, of Serafim of Sarov, who was known for his healing powers. Nicholas and the grand dukes who were present carried the coffin containing Serafim's remains, and both he and Alexandra bathed in the waters of a nearby stream that were considered holy because the saint had often bathed there. Nicholas strongly supported this glorification, a testament to the couple's desperate desire to produce a son and heir.[98] Their prayers were answered in 1904 with the birth of Tsarevich Aleksei.

Afflicted with the hereditary disease hemophilia, the young boy was often in pain. In 1912 he suffered one of his worst attacks, and his parents feared for his life. He received "piles of telegrams, icons with wishes for the darling's recovery."[99] A small icon with a gold *oklad*, or cover, with emeralds affixed to the halo was one such gift sent by the nuns of the Saint John of Ryla Convent (fig. 31).

As the result of what Nicholas and Alexandra considered to be the miracle of their son's birth, Saint Serafim became the protector of the imperial family, and they placed his relics in the new crypt chapel named after him in the

---

97. For more about this committee, see Robert L. Nichols, "The Icon and the Machine in Russia's Religious Renaissance 1900–1909," in *Christianity and the Arts in Russia*, ed. William Brumfield and Milos M. Velimirovic (Cambridge: Cambridge University Press, 1991), 131–44, and Oleg Tarasov, "The Russian Icon and the Culture of the *Modern*: The Renaissance of Popular Icon Painting in the Reign of Nicholas II," in *Experiment 7, The New Style: Russian Perceptions of Art Nouveau*, ed. Wendy R. Salmond (2001), 35–88.

98. For more on this event and its implications, see Robert L. Nichols, "The Friends of God: Nicholas II and Alexandra at the Canonization of Serafim of Sarov, July 1903," in *Religious and Secular Forces in Late Tsarist Russia*, ed. Charles E. Timberlake (Seattle: University of Washington Press, 1992), 206–303. See also Gregory L. Freeze, "Subversive Piety: Religion and Political Crisis in Late Imperial Russia," *Journal of Modern History* 68 (June 1996), 312–29, and Wortman, 2: 384–97.

99. Bing, 227.

Fig. 32. Northeast wall of the cave chapel in the Sovereigns' Fedorovskii Cathedral
From *Feodorovskii Gosudarev Sobor v Tsarskom Sele*
(Sovereigns' Fedorovskii Cathedral in Tsarskoe Selo), 1915
Hillwood Museum and Gardens Art Library

Fedorovskii Gosudarev Cathedral (the Sovereigns' Fedorovskii Cathedral) at Tsarskoe Selo (fig. 32). The construction of the cathedral (1909–12) and its surrounding *gorodok* (little town) was the most extensive building project with which Nicholas was personally involved during his reign.[100] With the imperial family's permanent residence now at Tsarskoe Selo, their support regiments, especially His Majesty's Own Combined Infantry and Convoy, required suitable housing and amenities. Unlike most other regiments, these did not have their own church. In 1908 Nicholas selected a site not far from the Alexander Palace for the new cathedral, and ground breaking occurred the

100. For a history of the building of the Fedorovskii Cathedral and the Fedorovskii *gorodok*, see Evgeniia Kirichenko, "Tsarskoe Selo in the Early Twentieth Century: An Expression of Nicholas II's Idea of Popular Monarchy," in *Experiment* 7, 19–71. In Kirichenko's opinion, "The new ensemble . . . initially took shape by degrees and not, it would seem, at Nicholas II's initiative, but merely with his consent and with the support of his innermost circle. Nicholas lacked that drive and initiative for working out building programs that had been so characteristic of his predecessors, especially Peter I, Catherine II, and Nicholas I" (see page 40).

next year. The church, designed by Vladimir Pokrovskii, was to be in the Russian style, using the fifteenth-century Annunciation Cathedral in the Moscow Kremlin as a prototype. Gradually a whole village, the Fedorovskii *gorodok*, grew up around the cathedral and included residences for the clergy. Architecturally, these structures were inspired by sixteenth-century monastic buildings.

World War I naturally created the need for nursing care and a massive number of hospital beds. Every available space, including palace halls, was turned into a hospital ward. In the spirit of the construction going on at the Fedorovskii *gorodok*, a cave chapel, in the form of a church in the early Christian catacombs, was added to the Court Hospital in the town of Tsarskoe Selo. This hospital became one of many under the protection of Alexandra, who was a great supporter of hospital and nursing care and even established a school for nurses at Tsarskoe Selo in 1905.

Silvio Danini, who became a court architect in 1911, drew the plans for the chapel, which was consecrated on 26 October 1914 and dedicated to Saints Constantine and Helen.[101] Sergei Vashkov, who had undertaken other commissions for Nicholas and Alexandra, designed a liturgical set with a chalice (fig. 33).[102] In addition to being an architect, Vashkov worked as the chief designer for the Moscow firm of Olovianishnikov and Sons. The firm stood out as the premier workshop for the production of liturgical plate in the neo-Russian style. Although Vashkov frequently drew on the styles of church art of the sixteenth and seventeenth centuries, this liturgical set is distinguished by its Byzantine origins. It perfectly suited the chapel, which, according to Alexandra, had been created in "the purest and ancient Byzantine style."[103] A glass bowl replaces the bowl of sardonyx or agate that was more commonly found in Byzantine chalices. Vashkov substituted the gold mounts set with

---

101. *Svetil'nik* 10 (1914), 29, and S.N. Vil'chkovskii, *Tsarskoe Selo* (St. Petersburg: Titul, 1911; reprint, 1992), iv, and a letter from Alexandra to Nicholas dated 21 October 1914, quoted in Joseph T. Fuhrmann, *The Complete Correspondence of Tsar Nicholas II and Empress Alexandra April 1914–March 1917* (Westport, Conn.: Greenwood Press, 1999), 28. According to Alexandra, a chapel had existed in this spot in the time of Catherine the Great. In fact, Danini designed two chapels, and Vashkov provided designs of liturgical sets for both. The other was in the hospital of the Red Cross Society. This chapel was consecrated on 1 October, three weeks before the cave chapel. I wish to thank Stephen de Angelis for his help in sorting out the confusion of these two chapels.

102. For other examples from this set, see *Svetil'nik* 10 (1914), figs. 15–25. Most of this set appears to have survived, including another chalice, and is now in the Russian Museum. See *Zolotaia kladovaia Russkogo muzeia: k 100-letiiu muzeia 1898–1998* (St. Petersburg: Palace Editions, 1998), ills. 202 and 203.

103. Fuhrmann, 28.

33. Chalice, ca. 1914
Firm of Olovianishnikov and Sons, Sergei Vashkov, designer
Silver, glass, enamel, ivory, semiprecious stones
Hillwood Museum and Gardens (cat. 83)

Fig. 34. Panagia, 1908–17
Firm of Olovianishnikov and Sons, Sergei Vashkov, designer
Silver gilt, aquamarines, peridots, amethysts, sapphires, mother-of-pearl
On loan to Middlebury College Museum of Art (cat. 82)

cloisonné-enameled plaques found in Byzantine examples with a simple enameled band decorated with white doves.[104]

Vashkov also designed for Olovianishnikov a panagia that shares with the chalice the feature of semiprecious stones hanging from small chains (fig. 34).[105] An image of the Vladimir Mother of God painted on mother-of-pearl forms the central feature of this piece, which a bishop wore around his neck. The panagia and the chalice fulfill one of Vashkov's goals in that they represent the most contemporary synthesis of traditional form and function with neo-Russian sensibility. In an introduction to a volume illustrating ten years of his work for the Olovianishnikov firm, Vashkov wrote that he did not "consider it necessary to copy slavishly the ancient forms of art," but rather he

104. See *Treasury of San Marco Venice* (Milan: Olivetti, 1984), 136 and 166, for eleventh-century chalices with bands set with cloisonné enamel plaques but with rings that were presumably intended for chains. The Cathedral of San Marco was featured in an article in *Svetil'nik* 4–5 (1913), 3–15, the year before this chalice was made. It included one of the chalices in the treasury.

105. This panagia is illustrated in Sergei Vashkov, *Religioznoe iskusstvo. Sbornik rabot tserkovnoi i grazhdanskoi utvari ispolnennoi tovarishchestvom* P. I. Olovianishnikova (Moscow: n.p., 1911), plate *zd* in Old Church Slavonic.

strived "to revive only the previous religious-moral ideals."[106] One senses here the confidence that Russian artists must have felt. No longer chained to historicist styles, they were innovatively melding all the influences that had been streaming into Russia in the last ten centuries.

THE RUSSIAN STYLE AND THE PROJECTION OF RUSSIA ABROAD

By the reign of Nicholas II in the 1890s, Moscow had become a revitalized and vibrant city. An increasingly important industrial center following the emancipation of the serfs, the city was home to a rapidly growing merchant class that was proud of its national heritage. By the early twentieth century many of these wealthy businessmen had made vast fortunes in textiles, railroads, or banking. They actively supported charities, founded musical and literary societies, funded educational institutions, contributed to museums, and established themselves as collectors of everything from icons and ancient Russian decorative arts to Russian paintings and works by the French impressionists. As an example of their appetite for collecting, about half the contributions to an exhibition of decorative arts from private collections held in Moscow in 1901 derived from merchant families.[107] These new Russian businessmen were increasingly in contact with the West and were beginning to lose their sense of cultural inferiority.[108]

Although the Russian style was slipping in favor by the early twentieth century, it had enjoyed a long and popular run. It was most successful when merged with Western art nouveau and secessionist ornament to create a new

---

106. Vashkov, introduction, unpaginated.

107. For more on the Moscow merchants and industrialists, see John Bowlt, "The Moscow Art Market," in *Between Tsar and People. Educated Society and the Quest for Public Identity in Late Imperial Russia*, ed. Edith W. Clowes, Samuel D. Kassow, and James L. West (Princeton: Princeton University Press, 1991), 110. The Moscow exhibition was held at the Stroganov School for the Applied Arts under the patronage of Grand Duchess Elizaveta Fedorovna, sister of the empress. See D. Nikiforov, *Sokrovischa v Moskve* (Moscow: Universitetskaia tipografiia, 1901). Alexandra Fedorovna sponsored another exhibition of decorative art that was held in 1904 at the Stieglitz School. Many merchants loaned objects on this occasion. See Adrian Prakhov, *Al'bom istoricheskoi vystavki predmetov iskusstva ustroennoi v 1904 g. v S.-Peterburge* (St. Petersburg: T-vo R. Golike and A. Vil'borg, 1907).

108. See "Introduction: The Problem of the Middle in Late Imperial Russian Society," in Kassow, West, and Clowes, 8–9. Elizabeth Kridl Valkenier gives a nuanced description of the Moscow elite and how it used its patronage in chapter 4 of her book on Valentin Serov. See also Joseph C. Bradley, "Merchant Moscow after Hours: Voluntary Associations and Leisure," in *Merchant Moscow. Images of Russia's Vanished Bourgeoisie*, ed. James L. West and Iurii A. Petrov (Princeton: Princeton University Press, 1998), 133–43, and Constantin Stanislavski, *My Life in Art* (New York: Meridian Books, 1956), chapters 1 and 2.

Fig. 35. Box with a painting after *The Boyar* by Konstantin Makovskii, ca. 1913
Firm of Fabergé, Fedor Rückert, workmaster. Silver gilt, enamel
Hillwood Museum and Gardens (cat. 94)

Russian style, as seen in the works by Vashkov. Russian style ornament was always most appropriately employed in the metal arts and the graphic arts—see the coronation menu by Vasnetsov (fig. 8)—because much of it derived from pre-Petrine metalwork or manuscript illuminations. Many paintings, such as Vasnetsov's *The Bogatyrs* (1898) and *Warrior at the Crossroads* (1882), focused on the legends of the ancient Russian warriors of Kievan Rus. Konstantin Makovskii's *A Boyar Wedding Feast* of 1883 (cat. 84) was inspired by the romantic view of the boyars' life in seventeenth-century Moscow, then being glamorized in numerous literary and musical sources. This was the very world that Peter, who saw no romance in the brutal politics of the boyars, had hoped to escape.

Another painting by Makovskii, *The Boyar*, decorates a box that Fedor Rückert created for the firm of Fabergé (fig. 35). Painted in 1913 for the Tercentenary, it appeared on the cover of *Sol'ntse Rossii* (The Sun of Russia) in

March of that year.[109] Costumes and characters reappear from Makovskii's early works, especially *A Boyar Wedding Feast*. This figure closely resembles the boyar who proposes a toast in the wedding scene. The box reveals the evolution of Russian enamels from the late nineteenth to the early twentieth century. Rückert abandoned the traditional colors and leaf-and-vine motifs that Ovchinnikov had used on the tankard (see fig. 13). He turned instead to the abstract patterns, sometimes in the form of stylized trees, pine cones, flowers, and vines rendered in muted colors, that are characteristic of the neo-Russian style. The purpose of the twisted wires was no longer just to separate colors; now they could be wound into swirls and cross hatching to create patterns of their own. Rückert was famous for the matte enamel paintings with which he decorated boxes.[110] These romantic or realist paintings were stylistically unrelated to their enamel borders but were linked instead by their colors.

Most enameled objects were, of course, created for Russian consumption or were intended as gifts to foreigners. They were also widely shown at international expositions and increasingly were sold abroad.[111] In the 1880s Tiffany & Co. established a Russian section in its New York store, where enamels, niello ware, porcelain, lacquer boxes, and icons were sold. In 1883 Henry Hiller, who had lived for many years in Russia and had served as a consular agent for Siberia during the Lincoln administration, became Tiffany's representative primarily responsible for the purchase of enamels and silver in Russia.[112] While Hiller surely bought enamels and silver from other Russian makers, Antip Kuzmichev, who founded his firm in 1856, is one of two silversmiths known to have had "Made for Tiffany & Co." stamped on his works.[113] A Kuzmichev cup and saucer (fig. 36) sold through Tiffany is typical of the kind of object that was perfect for sale as a souvenir and was clearly never intended to be of practical use. The plique-à-jour enamel used to decorate the pieces has no metal backing behind the enamel support. This allows light to shine through but makes the objects inherently fragile.

---

109. See Sotheby's, London, 7 April 1989, lot 16, for a replica of the painting.

110. For more Rückert boxes, see Odom 1996, 158–67, and Anne Odom, "A Key to the Past: Fedor Rückert's Miniature Picture Gallery," *Apollo* 137, no. 371 (January 1993), 22–27.

111. For more on objects in the Russian style that were sold abroad, see Anne Odom, "*Russkii stil'*: The Russian Style for Export," *The Magazine Antiques* 163, no. 3 (March 2003), 102–107.

112. For more on Hiller, see his obituary in the *New York Times* (21 January 1926), and Norman E. Saul, *Concord and Conflict. The United States and Russia, 1867–1914* (Lawrence: University Press of Kansas, 1996), 280.

113. Hiller's relationship to Kuzmichev can be found in the Henry Winans Hiller Papers, collection 77, box 2, vol. 7, Manuscript Collections, G.W. Blunt Library, Mystic Seaport Museum, Mystic, Connecticut. Gustav Klingert's name has also been found on pieces stamped "Made for Tiffany & Co." but more rarely.

Fig. 36. Cup and saucer, 1893
Firm of Antip Kuzmichev, made for Tiffany & Co.
Silver gilt, enamel
Private collection (cat. 91)

International expositions provided opportunities for firms such as Ovchinnikov and Khlebnikov to introduce their wares to a wider audience. Both showed their works to great acclaim at the Philadelphia Centennial Exposition in 1876 and at the World's Columbian Exposition in Chicago in 1893, where one of the American commissioners singled out Ovchinnikov's work for the highest praise. He noted that the firm showed a collection of "opaque enameled objects, in ancient Byzantine style, very noticeable from the beauty of the forms and the great richness of the coloring."[114] A certain irony can be attached to the popularity of the Russian style abroad. Foreigners neither knew nor cared that it reflected Russian efforts to rediscover their native ornament and design. They viewed the Russian style just the same as they did Byzantine, Persian, or Turkish ornament; its appeal was its exotic color and foreign designs. At these international expositions each country tried to differentiate itself by exhibiting wares that were obviously distinctive. The Russian style perfectly suited this requirement, and it continued to be exhibited long after it had lost its novelty.

One Russian factory already firmly established in the United States at the time of the 1893 Chicago fair was that of the Brothers Kornilov. Founded in St. Petersburg in 1839, the factory participated in the Philadelphia Centennial Exposition in 1876. Precisely when Kornilov began to sell its wares through Tiffany & Co. is unclear, but it appears that it was doing so at least by 1883.[115]

In addition to Tiffany, Kornilov sold Russian-style porcelain to Bailey, Banks, and Biddle in Philadelphia; Shreeve, Crump, and Low in Boston; and Shreeve and Company in San Francisco, among other stores. The factory employed the services of several major illustrators of the day, including the realist artist Nikolai Karazin; Ivan Bilibin, who published artistic editions of Russian fairy tales and was associated with the World of Art group (cat. 100); and Elizaveta Bëm, whose enormously popular saccharine paintings of children in boyar costume spouting peasant proverbs were reproduced on postcards. Similar to the enamel borders around Rückert's miniature enamel paintings, the ornament on the rims of Kornilov plates was often stylistically unsuited to the painted scene in the center (cat. 97). The most sophisticated of the artists working for Kornilov was the architect Ivan Galnbek, who was

114. E. Crawford, "Enamels of all Nations, as Exhibited in the Columbian Exposition," *Report of the Committee on Awards of the World's Columbian Commission*, vol. I (Washington, D.C.: Government Printing Office, 1901), 304.

115. P.I. Glukhovskoi, *Otchet general'nago kommisara russkago otdela Vsemirnoi kolumbovoi vystavki v Shikago* (St. Petersburg: V. Kirshbaum, 1895), 30–31. The author states that at the time of the Chicago fair, Kornilov had already been selling objects in American stores for ten years.

employed as the librarian at the Stieglitz Central School for Technical Drawing in St. Petersburg. Galnbek provided the Kornilov Factory with drawings for new forms, like the sauce boat with its squared off perforated handles, and he also created several services, one decorated with birds (fig. 37) and another with fish.[116] In addition he produced designs for vases, soup tureens, and soup bowls with bears for handles. Like Vashkov, Galnbek transformed Russian motifs and love of ornament into a truly modern Russian style.

THE WORLD OF ART

The avant-garde movement that revolutionized Russian art grew out of this hothouse environment in Moscow after 1905. In St. Petersburg, however, in reaction to the realist painters of the 1860s and 1870s—the *Peredvizhniki*, or Wanderers—and the nationalism of the Russian style, a group of artists surrounding the energetic entrepreneur Sergei Diagilev turned to the glories of classical St. Petersburg and to Russia's links with the West. Truly imbued with Peter's dream, they wanted to reconnect with European culture.

Beginning in 1898 and lasting until 1904, the World of Art (*Mir iskusstva*) group published a journal of the same name, in which it included articles on Western and Russian artists and often introduced new talent. In 1902 Benois wrote an article on "Picturesque Petersburg," deploring the neglect Petersburg had suffered at the hands of artists and extolling the beauty of the city's classical architecture.[117] In the first of several articles he wrote on St. Petersburg, Benois argued that the city's architecture was not just a copy of Western elements. Clearly it had its own Russian flavor, which easily competed with that of any European capital in the first half of the nineteenth century. Underscoring his point were numerous splendid photographs of architectural details and woodcut illustrations by Evgenii Lancere and Anna Ostroumova-Lebedeva. These photographs and woodcuts would have been the stuff of Peter's dreams. Although of a later date, Ostroumova-Lebedeva's *Ships* (fig. 38) conveys the beauty and mystery of Peter's capital on the Neva.

In 1900 Diagilev's initial financing of the journal was not renewed. Valentin Serov, who at the time was painting a portrait of Nicholas, took the

---

116. For more of Galnbek's designs, see Tamara Kudrjawzewa, "Iwan Gallnbeck und russischer Stil im Kornilow-Porzellan," *Pinakoteke* 10–11 (1999), 115–21.

117. A. Benois, "Zhivopisnyi Peterburg," *Mir iskusstva* 1 (1902), 1–5. Benois, who founded the journal *Khudozhestvennye sokrovishcha Rossii*, featured portraits, engravings, and objects related to Peter in the January 1903 issue of this journal in celebration of the bicentenary.

Fig. 37. Sauce boat and plate, 1900–10
Factory of the Brothers Kornilov, Ivan Galnbek, designer
Hard-paste porcelain. Private collection (cat. 99)

opportunity at one of their many sittings to tell the emperor of Diagilev's plight. Although Nicholas considered the artworks of the World of Art group decadent, he contributed from his personal funds to support the journal's publication, probably until 1904.[118] The World of Art group also organized a number of exhibitions beginning in 1898. The emperor and various grand dukes regularly attended. In 1905 Diagilev secured paintings for a major exhibition of Russian historical portraits that was held in the Tauride Palace, the new home of the Duma, or parliament. The emperor and several members of his family graciously loaned paintings from the imperial collections. Diagilev himself, along with Grand Duke Nikolai Mikhailovich, who as head of the organizing committee had secured the palace as an exhibition space, led the emperor on a personal tour.[119]

The next year, in 1906, Diagilev decided to introduce Russian art to Paris. In the following years he produced programs of music and opera. He created a sensation in 1908 with his production of *Boris Godunov*, sung by Chaliapin, and in 1909 he stormed Paris with Russian ballet. The ballet *Le Pavillion d'Armide* and the Polovtsian ballet from the last act of *Prince Igor* appeared on the program of this first ballet season.

Le Pavillion d'Armide had been performed in St. Petersburg two years earlier, in 1907. Grand Duke Vladimir, who supported Diagilev in many of his ventures in Paris, was in the midst of obtaining permission for Diagilev to borrow the sets and costumes from the Mariinskii Theater, as he had done before, when he suddenly died. At the grand duke's laying out in the Vladimir Palace, Nicholas approached the distraught Diagilev. As Diagilev recalled, the emperor "came towards me, crossed himself, and gazing thoughtfully at me murmured, as if to himself, 'Yes, he was very fond of you.'"[120]

As a result of backstage politics, Diagilev's request for the sets and costumes was turned down. Benois, who had designed the original costumes, had to create a new set (fig. 39), but he felt that he had improved these by using the Sèvres colors of apple green, rose pink, and turquoise blue. By the early twentieth century an enthusiastic audience in the West had discovered Russian literature and music, but nothing cemented their appreciation of the creativity of Russian art like Diagilev's Ballets Russes.

---

118. Richard Buckle, *Diaghilev* (New York: Atheneum, 1984), 53; Valkenier, 127–28.

119. *Mir iskusstva* 5 (1904), 113. Benois, who was in Paris at the time, described with considerable disappointment what he had heard from Petersburg, namely, that "not by a single word did he [Nicholas] reveal his personal attitude to all he had seen, although it was so closely related to his person." Quoted in Buckle, 86. Nicholas did not even mention this exhibition in his diary; see *Dnevniki*, February 1905.

120. Quoted in Buckle, 131.

Fig. 38. *Ships*, 1917. Anna Ostroumova-Lebedeva. Color woodcut
The George Riabov Collection of Russian Art, Jane Voorhees Zimmerli Art Museum,
Rutgers, The State University of New Jersey (cat. 103)

Fig. 39. Costume design for a gentleman of the court, for *Le Pavillion d'Armide*, 1909
Alexander Benois. Watercolor on paper
The George Riabov Collection of Russian Art, Jane Voorhees Zimmerli Art Museum,
Rutgers, The State University of New Jersey (cat. 102)

From 1909 on, Diagilev devoted himself to projects in Paris, increasing interaction among Russian and Western artists, dancers, and composers, even though members of his circle continued to work in St. Petersburg. Benois' concern with historic St. Petersburg led him to play a leading role in efforts to preserve historic monuments and buildings in the city. As an example of their commitment, he and others formed in 1911 the Society for the Preservation and Protection of Russian Monuments of Art and Antiquity, and the next year they opened the Museum of Old Petersburg.[121] In fact, on a cultural level, no group more sincerely appreciated Peter's Westernization of Russia and the possibilities it generated for the future in the co-mingling of Russian and Western culture than Diagilev, Benois, and the World of Art artists.

WHAT DID BECOME OF PETER'S DREAM?

In 1905, shortly after the opening of the exhibition *Russian Historical Portraits*, Diagilev was celebrated at a dinner in Moscow. On that occasion he made a disturbing and prophetic speech. While collecting paintings in various country houses and palaces around Russia, he realized these estates were in decay and were "inhabited today by charming mediocre people who could no longer stand the strain of bygone parades." He went on:

> That is what completely convinced me that we live in a terrible period of transition. We are doomed to die to pave the way for the resurrection of a new culture, which will take from us what remains of our weary wisdom. . . .
>
> We are witnesses of the greatest moment of summing up in history, in the name of a new and unknown culture, which will be created by us, and which will also sweep us away. . . .[122]

Diagilev's world was indeed being swept away. Dynamic, young avant-garde artists would soon replace members of the World of Art, and the Bolsheviks would eventually wipe out imperial culture. Nicholas II, when not obsessed with the tragic illness of his son, was focused on his unrelenting adherence to autocratic rule and the revival of pre-Petrine Russian culture.

---

121. Katerina Clark, *Petersburg, Crucible of Cultural Revolution* (Cambridge: Harvard University Press, 1995), 60. Grand Duke Nikolai Mikhailovich was the president of this society.

122. Arnold L. Haskell, in collaboration with Walter Nouvel, *Diaghileff. His Artistic and Private Life* (New York: Simon and Schuster, 1935), 136.

Clearly he was in no position to make the reforms and meet the demands required of modernization in the twentieth century. Neither he nor members of his family forged contacts with the newly moneyed industrial elite, who might have become useful allies.[123] The record of Nicholas and his immediate advisors left little cause for hope, despite many positive signs in society that Russia could have modernized without a revolution.

Where does this survey leave us when we look back to Peter's hopes for Russia's luxury industries? How can we sum up the state of Russian court culture in the spring of 1914, just before the onslaught of war? First of all, the clientele for all luxury wares had dramatically changed by the early twentieth century. It was huge by comparison with what it had been in the eighteenth century. The ever-growing middle class was not averse to conspicuous consumption as newly rich businessmen furnished grand homes. They could afford lavish gifts for weddings and anniversaries. Even factory workers joined together to present elaborate gifts to their employers at the time of retirement.

Those firms that still produced primarily for the court, such as the Imperial Porcelain and Glass Factory, were mired in a bureaucracy that prevented them from exercising creative leadership and attracting the talents of avant-garde artists. Thus the artistic institutions that Peter and his immediate successors envisioned no longer enjoyed the prestige they had once commanded. On the other hand, healthy competition among jewelers, silversmiths, and private porcelain and glass factories, and the challenge posed by a growing arts and crafts movement, caused businesses to expand. Royal factories across Europe faced this phenomenon as international exhibitions heightened awareness of what everyone else was doing. Russia was immersed in this Western culture, this exchange of artistic ideas and new techniques. This is surely what Peter the Great would have wished.

Despite his fascination with Holland and his visits to England, Peter could not have advocated the political institutions of those countries in the early eighteenth century. Instead, he adopted the absolutism of Louis XIV, which by that time was already antiquated and about to collapse. Russia had successfully acquired the veneer of the West, but it was locked into a governmental system that teetered on the verge of revolution during the last two decades of the empire. If Peter's dream had been for Russia to develop into an integral part of western Europe, he partially succeeded. Russia had acquired the cultural veneer. Western Europe, and particularly France, did not modernize peacefully. Had World War I not occurred, and had Nicholas been

---

123. Lieven, 57.

forced into a constitutional monarchy (which, given his views, is highly un-likely), such political and artistic development might have been continuous, if not necessarily peaceful. The Russian Revolution, unfortunately, caused such a severe break that it ensured Russia would be left out of the mainstream both culturally and politically for the next seventy years.

Paradoxically, interest in pre-Revolutionary court culture and a fascination with the tragedy of the last imperial family constantly grows in the West. The brutal shooting of Nicholas and Alexandra and their children, as well as other members of the imperial family, has lent a special aura to the last emperor's reign, despite all its contradictions. We treasure these objects because of their personal connection to this horrific episode and for the way they illuminate the complicated nature of Russian society two hundred years after Peter founded his "window on the West."

Cat. 21. Goblet and wine glass, ca. 1910–17
Imperial Porcelain and Glassworks, Lavr Orlovskii, engraver. Glass enamel
Hillwood Museum and Gardens

Checklist of the Exhibition

Notes on silver marks: *crossed anchors is the mark for St. Petersburg before 1896; St. George and the dragon is the mark for Moscow before 1896; kokoshnik facing left is the mark for 1896–1908; kokoshnik facing right is the mark for 1908–1917; 56 is a mark for the gold standard; 84, 88, and 91 are marks for the silver standard (91 is the equivalent of sterling and used by the Russians primarily for export); imperial warrant indicates the maker's mark appears with the double-headed eagle, usually above it.* This means the firm was a purveyor to the court.

All objects designated "On loan to Middlebury College Museum of Art" are from the collection of Nancy and Edward Wynkoop.

1. Peter the Great

Russia, 1714
Engraving after Johann Gottfried Tannauer (Dannhauer) (1680–1737)
H. 14⅛ in. (36 cm), W. 9⅝ in. (24.5 cm)
The George Riabov Collection of Russian Art, Jane Voorhees Zimmerli Art Museum, Rutgers, The State University of New Jersey,
PG 1999.1148

Inscription in Russian: *Peter the Great, Emperor and Autocrat of the Fatherland of All the Russias;* and in Latin: *Petrus Magnus Totius Russie Imperator et Autocrator Pater Patriae*

2. Second Winter Palace

Russia, ca. 1753
Engraving after a drawing by Mikhail Makhaev (1718–1770); Grigorii Kachalov (1711–1759), engraver
H. 22 in. (55.8 cm), W. 30 in. (76.2 cm)
Hillwood Museum and Gardens, 55.91
Museum Purchase 1998

Inscription in Russian: *Prospekt starago zimniago dvortsa c kanalom soediniaiushim Moiky s Nevoiu* [View of the Old Winter Palace with the canal linking the Moika with the Neva]; and in French: *Vüe de l'ancien Palais d'hiver de la Majesté Imperiale et du canal qui joint la Moika avec la Neva*

During the reign of Elizabeth I (r. 1741–1761), Makhaev produced two series of drawings of St. Petersburg. This engraving derives from the first series drawn in 1753 to commemorate the fiftieth anniversary of the founding of the city. To the left is the second Winter Palace, built between 1719 and 1721 after designs by Georg Mattarnovi and enlarged in 1726 and 1727, possibly by Domenico Trezzini.

3. Anichkov Palace and the Nevskii Prospect

Russia, ca. 1753
Engraving after a drawing by Mikhail Makhaev (1717–1780);
Grigorii Kachalov (1711–1759), engraver
H. 22 in. (55.8 cm), W. 30 in. (76.2 cm)
Hillwood Museum and Gardens, 55.87
Museum Purchase 1998

Inscription in Russian: *Prospekt novopostroennykh palat protiv Anichkovskikh vorot ot vostochnoi storony s chastiiu Sanktpeterburga i Nevskoi perspektivoi dorogi ot reki fontanki* [View of the newly built palace opposite the Anichkov Gate from the eastern side with part of St. Petersburg and the Nevskii perspective road from the River Fontanka]; and in French: *Vüe du Nouveau Palais près de la porte triomphale d'Anitschki vers l'orient avec une partie de la ville & du chemin du Monastère d'Alexandre Newski prise du Coté de la Fontanka*

Architects Mikhail G. Zemtsov and G.D. Dmitriev designed the Anichkov Palace for Elizabeth I, and it was built in the 1740s. By Elizabeth's time, St. Petersburg had expanded along three roads leading away from the Admiralty toward the river Fontanka. Nicholas II grew up in the Anichkov Palace, seen here on the left, and it remained the main residence of his mother, Maria Fedorovna, until 1917.

4. Four photogravures from the Boyar Ball, 1903

Al'bom kostiumirovannago bala v Zimnem dvortse v fevrale 1903 g. [Album of the costume ball in the Winter Palace in February 1903] (St. Petersburg, 1904)
Each mounted H. 11 in. (28 cm), W. 5¹⁵/₁₆ in. (15.1 cm)

Hillwood Museum and Gardens Art Library,
Dunning Collection

4a. Emperor Nicholas II in the costume of Tsar
Aleksei Mikhailovich. Photogravure from a
photograph by Levitskii, no. I

4b. Empress Alexandra in the costume of Maria
Miloslavskaia. Photogravure from a photograph by Levitskii, no. II

4c. Grand Duchess Maria Georgievna in the costume of a peasant woman from Torzhok in
the time of Tsar Aleksei Mikhailovich. Photogravure from a photograph by Boissonas
and F. Eggler, no. XV

4d. Grand Duke Georgii Mikhailovich in the
costume of a seventeenth-century boyar.
Photogravure from a photograph by Levitskii, no. XIV

5. Portrait of Nicholas II

St. Petersburg, 1912
Mikhail V. Rundaltsov (1871–1935)
Pastel on paper
H. 16 in. (40.6 cm), W. 12¼ in. (31.1 cm)
Hillwood Museum and Gardens, 52.9

Signed in Cyrillic: *Rundaltsov 1912*

This painting hung in the Russian embassy in
Paris at the time of the Revolution.

6. Portrait of Alexandra Fedorovna

St. Petersburg, ca. 1894–96
Oil on canvas
H. 29⅛ in. (74 cm), W. 21¾ in. (55.2 cm)
Hillwood Museum and Gardens, 51.81

7. Portrait of Nicholas II

Russia, 1896
Lithograph on silk
Sight: H. 19⅛ in. (48.6 cm), W. 15½ in.
(39.4 cm)
On loan to Middlebury College Museum of Art,
L 110.1993

Inscription: *S.M. Le Tsar Nicolas II*

This image of Nicholas II and the next one of his
wife Alexandra appear to have been taken from
an illustration in the coronation volume (cat. 14)
from a drawing by E. Samokish-Sudkovskaia,
one of the artists who was invited to attend the
coronation.

8. Portrait of Alexandra Fedorovna

Russia, 1896
Lithograph on silk
Sight: H. 19⅛ in. (48.6 cm), W. 15½ in.
(39.4 cm)
On loan to Middlebury College Museum of Art,
L 111.1993

Inscription: *S.M. La Tsarine Aleksandra Fedorovna*

Lithographs on silk, such as this and the previous one of Nicholas, were a popular means of
distributing their portraits to a wide audience.

9. Announcement of the coronation of
Nicholas and Alexandra

Moscow, 1896
Colored lithograph after a drawing by Ivan
Petrov-Ropet (1845–1908); A.A. Levinson,
printers
H. 16 in. (40.5 cm), L. 11 in. (28 cm)
The George Riabov Collection of Russian Art,
Jane Voorhees Zimmerli Art Museum, Rutgers,
The State University of New Jersey, Ralph and
Barbara Voorhees Purchase Fund, 1995.0213

10. Coronation menu

Moscow, 1896
Colored lithograph after a drawing by
Viktor Vasnetsov (1848–1926); A.A. Levinson,
printers
H. 36 in. (91.4 cm), W. 12 in. (30.5 cm)
Hillwood Museum and Gardens, 55.22

Inscription in Russian: at the top: *The Holy
Coronation of the Sovereign Emperor Nicholas II
and the Sovereign Empress Alexandra Feodorovna*

The menu: *Soup/ Pickled Cucumber Soup/ Borscht/
Pâtés/ Steamed Sterlet/ Lamb/ Entrée:/ Capons/
Salad/ Asparagus/ Pheasant in Aspic/ Dessert:/
Fruits in wine/ ice cream*

Below that: *Glory to God in the heavens, praise to/
our sovereigns on this earth/ Glory to all the Russian people/ Glory to his faithful servants/ Glory to
his distinguished guests/ Glory! May truth be in
Russia a shining/ glory more fair than the sun*

At the bottom: *And this song we sing to bread,/
we sing to bread. We render/ honor to bread. Glory
to the / old people for consolation, to/ good people
for listening to, Glory/ Glory forever/ and ever/
Glory!*

This menu, rolled up, graced the place of each person attending the coronation banquet, held in the Faceted Hall in the Kremlin.

11. *Felon'* (chasuble)

Moscow, 1896
Sapozhnikov and Company
Silk brocade, gold and silver threads
H. 59 in. (150 cm)
Hillwood Museum and Gardens, 44.9

This *felon'* is part of a large set of vestments made for the coronation of Nicholas II. A vestment created for Patriarch Adrian in 1696, two hundred years earlier, served as a prototype.

12. Bread and salt dish

Russia, 1894–96
A. Glazunova, painter
Faience
D. 17¹³/₁₆ in. (45 cm)
Hillwood Museum and Gardens, 27.4

Marks: impressed mark for an unknown factory

Signed in Cyrillic: *A Glazunova*

This dish was possibly made for the coronation of Nicholas and Alexandra. Their combined monograms appear in the center with the imperial double-headed eagle above. At the top is the personal coat of arms of the emperor, with a crown of a king overall. Balancing this is the coat of arms of St. Petersburg on the bottom left and that of Moscow on the right.

13. Coronation cup

Moscow, 1896
Enamel on metal, gilding
H. 4⅛ in. (10.5 cm), Dia. 3¹³/₁₆ in. (9.7 cm)
On loan to Middlebury College Museum of Art, L 98.1993

Monogram in Cyrillic: *N II* and *A* for Nicholas II and Alexandra, and the year *1896*

Intended for beer, this cup is one of many distributed at a celebration at the Khodynka Field in Moscow following Nicholas II's coronation. Numerous people were trampled as they rushed over a rough and uneven field to get a souvenir cup.

14. *Koronatsionnyi sbornik*, volumes I and II

St. Petersburg, 1899
Ekspeditsiia zagotovleniia gos. bumag, publisher
N. Samokish, designer of cover
Each H. 17½ in. (44.5 cm), W. 13½ in. (34.3 cm), D. 2 in. (5.1 cm)
Hillwood Museum and Gardens Art Library

This two-volume luxury album was produced for the coronation of Nicholas II. At least 1,300 of these albums were published in Russian and another 350 in French.

15. Tercentenary plates

Moscow, ca. 1913
Firm of Fabergé
Anders Nevaleinen (1858–1933), workmaster
Silver
L 115.1993: Dia. 5⅛ in. (13.1 cm)
L 116.1993: Dia. 6⁵/₁₆ in. (16.1 cm)
On loan to Middlebury College Museum of Art

Marks: L 115.1993: kokoshnik facing right; alpha for St. Petersburg; *84*; *K. Fabergé* in Cyrillic with the imperial warrant; *AN* for Anders Nevaleinen

L 116.1993: kokoshnik facing left; *AR* in Cyrillic for St. Petersburg assayer A. Rikhter; *K. Fabergé* in Cyrillic with imperial warrant; *AN* for Anders Nevaleinen

Engraved inscription in Russian on the larger plate (L 116.1993): *To Her Highness Grand Duchess Mariia Georgievna on the day of the 300th anniversary of the rule of the House of Romanov from faithful officials of the court 1613–1913*
Engraved inscription in Russian on the smaller plate (L 115.1993) is the same but is addressed to *Her Highness Ksenia Georgievna*

16. Pendant

St. Petersburg, 1913
Silver gilt, purpurite, diamonds, rubies, emeralds
H. 1½ in. (3.8 cm), W. ¹¹/₁₆ in. (1.8 cm)
On loan to Middlebury College Museum of Art, L 82.1993

The pendant takes the shape of the Cap of Monomakh, the ancient crown of Russia and a symbol of the Tercentenary.

17. Tercentenary brooch

St. Petersburg, 1913
Firm of Fabergé
Albert Holmström (1876–1925), workmaster
Gold, aquamarine, rubies, diamonds
Dia. 1³/₁₆ in. (3.1 cm)
Hillwood Museum and Gardens, 17.84

Marks: *kokoshnik* facing right; alpha for St.
Petersburg; *56*; *AH* for Albert Holmström;
inventory number *4595*

Members of the court received brooches and
pins at the celebration of the Tercentenary of
Romanov rule in 1913. They were also presented to deserving citizens in the course of the
year. Any pins left over were distributed in
1914. This pin was awarded to the actress
Maria Vedrinskaia of the Imperial Theaters on
2 July 1914.

18. Tercentenary cross

St. Petersburg, 1913
Firm of Rudolf Veide
Silver gilt, enamel
H. 2⅝ in. (6.6 cm), W. 1½ in. (3.8 cm)
Hillwood Museum and Gardens, 18.66

Marks: *kokoshnik* facing right; alpha for St. Petersburg; *88*; *RV* in Cyrillic for Rudolf Veide

Inscription in Russian on back: *The Tsars Rule
Through God*; the initials *M* and *N II* in Cyrillic
for Tsars Michael and Nicholas II; the Slavonic
letters *A Kh G I* and *A Ts G I* for the Slavonic
numerals 1613–1913

This cross was a jubilee award presented on 21
February 1913 by the Holy Synod to all members of the clergy, both black and white, who
were in service at the time of the three-hun-
dredth anniversary of the house of Romanov.

19. Plate

Moscow, 1913
Imperial Stroganov School
Silver gilt, enamel
Dia. 9⁷/₁₆ in. (24 cm)
Private collection

Marks: *kokoshnik* facing right; delta for
Moscow; *88*; *ISU* in Cyrillic for Imperial
Stroganov School

Inscription in Russian: *Kostroma 1613 / From
Grand Duchess Elizaveta Feodorovna / Moscow 1913*

Enameled paintings of the Ipatiev Monastery
in Kostroma, where Michael Romanov lived
before he was called to Moscow, and the Moscow Kremlin enliven the plate.

20. Dessert plate from the Kremlin Service

St. Petersburg, 1837–55
Imperial Porcelain Factory
Fedor Solntsev (1801–1892), designer
Hard-paste porcelain
Dia. 8⅝ in. (21.9 cm)
Hillwood Museum and Gardens, 25.314.1

Marks: *N I* in underglaze blue for the period
of Nicholas I (r. 1825–1855); Kremlin Armory
inventory number *OXP 21905*

Fedor Solntsev created the designs for the
Kremlin Service in 1837. Nicholas I personally
directed that the service be created in the "old
Russian taste," the first expression of the Russian revival style in the decorative arts. The
design derives from a gold and enamel plate
produced by the Kremlin Armory workshops
for Tsar Aleksei in 1667. The service was regularly used at coronations, and additions were
made for the Tercentenary of Romanov rule
in 1913.

21. Goblet and wineglass

St. Petersburg, ca. 1910–17
Imperial Porcelain and Glassworks
Lavr Orlovskii, engraver
Glass, enamel
Goblet: H. 8³/₁₆ in. (20.8 cm)
Wineglass: H. 6⁹/₁₆ in. (16.7 cm)
Hillwood Museum and Gardens,
23.129.1 and .3

Engraved in Cyrillic *NA II* for Nicholas II
Aleksandrovich

In 1912 Nicholas II commissioned a large
number of glasses in all sizes for the celebration of the Tercentenary the following year.
They were additions to an existing service in
the style of goblets made in the reign of
Elizabeth I (1741–1761).

22. Tercentenary menu

Moscow, 1913
Colored lithograph after a drawing by Sergei
Iaguzhinskii (1862–1947); A.A. Levinson,
printers
H. 17 in. (44.6 cm), W. 6⁵/₁₆ in. (16 cm)
Hillwood Museum and Gardens, 55.24

Text in Russian: *1613–1913*
House of Romanovs
On scroll to left: *Truth and Charity*
On shield to right: *For Faith, Tsar, and
Fatherland*
In between: *Abundance and earthly fruits*
25 May 1913
Moscow
Dinner
Soups: Turtle and a purée of chicken with asparagus
Pirozhki
Sterlet 'Imperial'
Saddle of wild goat with garnish
Chicken with truffles
Punch 'Victoria'
Entrée: Duck and capon
Salad with cucumbers
Asparagus with sauce
Peaches 'Cardinal'
Ice cream 'Parisian'
Dessert
The Caterer of the Court of His Highness

23. Tankard

Moscow, 1890
Firm of Ovchinnikov
Silver gilt, enamel
H. 6¾ in. (17.2 cm)
Hillwood Museum and Gardens, 15.44

Marks: St. George and the dragon; *LO* in Cyrillic for assayer Lev Fedorovich Oleks; *88*; *1890*;
P. Ovchinnikov in Cyrillic with imperial
warrant

The tankard was possibly a gift from the city
of St. Petersburg to the officers of the French
squadrons that visited the city in 1897.

24. Dame à Portrait

St. Petersburg, 1894–1917
Carl Blank
Gold, paste, miniatures
H. 3⁷/₁₆ in. (8.7 cm), W. 2⅞ in. (7.2 cm)

Hillwood Museum and Gardens, 18.65

Marks: *E.T.*, a French mark stamped on foreign objects made in an alloy below the French
standard

Countess Ekaterina Pavlovna Sheremeteva received this badge when she was appointed
lady-in-waiting in 1912. In this honorary position she served both Maria Fedorovna, the
mother of Nicholas II, and his wife, Alexandra
Fedorovna. That the double portrait is set with
paste diamonds instead of real ones was not
uncommon. The prestige of the award lies in
its symbolic meaning rather than its monetary
value. A dame à portrait was the highest
honor an empress could bestow on her ladies-
in-waiting (*stats-dama*).[1]

---

[1]. I am grateful to Ulla Tillander-Godenhielm for iden-
tifying the recipient from the numbers *333* and *334* on
the back of the miniatures.

25. Pendant watch

St. Petersburg, ca. 1901
Gold, diamonds, enamel
Dia. of watch ⅞ in. (2.1 cm), H. of whole 3⁷/₁₆
in. (8.7 cm)
Hillwood Museum and Gardens, 16.18.1–.2

Marks: kokoshnik facing left; *Ia L* in Cyrillic for
St. Petersburg assayer Iakov Lapunov; *56*;
stamped with model number *19483*

Inscribed: *Donné par S.M. L'Empereur à Melle
Barety. St. Petersburg 19 2/III 01*

The French actress Margarita Barety performed
at the Imperial Mikhailovskii Theater in St. Petersburg from 1898 to the 1904–1905 season.
This watch was probably presented to her for a
benefit performance held on 23 February
1901.

26. Presentation watch

St. Petersburg, ca. 1904
Firm of Pavel Bure (Paul Buhré)
Gold, enamel
H. 3 in. (7.6 cm), W. 2⅛ in. (5.4 cm)
Hillwood Museum and Gardens, 16.17.1

Marks: kokoshnik facing left; *56*; stamped with
the model number *79018* and *0,583* for the gold
standard

Inscribed inside in Russian: *Bure /With kindest regards to Archdeacon of the Court Cathedral I. Popov for officiating at the Holy Christening of His Highness the Heir Tsarevich Grand Duke Aleksei Nikolaevich 11 August 1904*

Buhré was a well-known Swiss firm that opened a shop in St. Petersburg in 1815. This type of watch commonly served as a presentation gift during the reign of Nicholas II. Popov was one of several members of the clergy that officiated on this occasion.

27. Presentation ashtray

St. Petersburg, ca. 1905
Firm of Carl Fabergé
Probably Anders Nevaleinen (1858–1933), workmaster
Silver gilt, enamel
H. $^{11}/_{16}$ in. (1.8 cm), W. 4¾ in. (12.1 cm)
Hillwood Museum and Gardens, 12.162

Marks: kokoshnik facing left; initials *Ia L* in Cyrillic for St. Petersburg assayer Iakov Lapunov; *K. Fabergé* in Cyrillic; partially legible *AN* for Anders Nevaleinen;[2] inventory number 12511; on front of coin, mostly abbreviated in Russian: *By the Grace of God, Catherine II, Empress and Autocrat St. Petersburg*; on the reverse in Russian: *Coin Ruble 1772* and the initials *A Sh* for Aleksei Schneze (act. 1766–72), the moneyer, or mint master

Engraved on back: *VIII.1905.IX* and *C.N. Portsmouth*

The ashtray is set with a one-ruble coin, dated 1772, from the reign of Catherine II. It was probably presented to Konstantin (Constantine, thus C.N.) Nabokov, secretary for the Russian delegation sent to Portsmouth, New Hampshire, to conclude the treaty that ended the Russo-Japanese War. The treaty was signed on 5 September 1905, three days before the date on the ashtray. Nabokov, the uncle of the writer Vladimir Nabokov, was later counselor of the Russian embassy in Washington.

---

2. Anders Nevaleinen's initials sometimes appear, as they do on several of these works, with the Moscow mark of Fabergé and sometimes with the mark of a Petersburg assayer and sometimes with a Moscow one.

28. Commemorative plaque

St. Petersburg, ca. 1905
Firm of Fabergé
Anders Nevaleinen (1858–1933), workmaster
Silver
H. 4 in. (10.2 cm), W. 6¹/₁₆ in. (15.4 cm)
Hillwood Museum and Gardens, 12.159

Marks: kokoshnik facing left; *91*; *AR* in Cyrillic for the Petersburg assayer A. Rikhter; *K. Fabergé* in Cyrillic with the imperial warrant; *AN* for Anders Nevaleinen

Inscription engraved in Russian on the front: "*Cruiser First Class Rank 'Riurik' of 15200 tons displacement and 19700 horsepower. Keel laid in Barrow-in-Furness (England) in the works of Vickers and Co. on 9(22) August 1905.*" On the reverse is inscribed: "*Administrative head of the Navy Ministry General Adjutant F.K. Avelan. Chairman of the Technical Council General Adjutant V.F. Dubasov. Head of the Main Shipbuilding Department Counter-Admiral A.R. Rodionov. Principal Shipbuilding Inspector Lieutenant General N.E. Kuteinikov. Shipbuilding Inspector Engineer K.A. Tennison.*"

The Riurik was launched on 17 November 1905. It participated in action as part of the Baltic Fleet in World War I. Such plaques were presented to dignitaries at the laying of the keel.

29. Vase

St. Petersburg, 1907
Imperial Porcelain Factory
Hard-paste porcelain
H. 17½ in. (44.5 cm), Dia. 12½ in. (31.8 cm)
On loan to Middlebury College Museum of Art, L 25.1995

Marks: *N II* in Cyrillic in underglaze green for the period of Nicholas II (r. 1894–1917)

The vase came with a paper note saying that it was a gift from Nicholas II to the mayor of Vologda in "remembrance of a visit by Nicholas II to the Church of Saraphim Sarovskii to give thanks for birth of Tsarevich" (unverified).

30. Two pieces from the Purple Service

St. Petersburg, 1905, 1908
Imperial Porcelain Factory

Hard-paste porcelain
Dessert plate (25.393.1): Dia. 9 in. (22.9 cm)
Salad bowl (25.394): W. 9³/16 in. (23.3 cm),
D. 9³/16 in. (23.3 cm)
Hillwood Museum and Gardens

Marks: dessert plate: *N II* in Cyrillic and *1905* in
underglaze green; salad bowl: *N II* in Cyrillic
and *1908* in underglaze green

This service, also called the Tsarkoselskii Service, was created for use at Tsarskoe Selo.

31. Champagne and wine glass

St. Petersburg, late 19th–early 20th century
Imperial Glassworks
Glass
Champagne: H. 6⁵/16 in. (16 cm)
Wine: H. 5⁵/16 in. (13.5 cm)
From the collection of Mr. and Mrs. Set
Charles Momjian

Each piece is engraved in Cyrillic with *NA* for
Nikolai Aleksandrovich, the future Nicholas II.

32. Two tumblers from the imperial yacht
Polar Star

St. Petersburg, ca. 1888
Imperial Glassworks
Glass
Purple (L 112.1993): H. 2¹/16 in. (8 cm), Dia.
1½ in. (3.8 cm)
Turquoise (L 113.1993): H. 4¼ in. (10.8 cm),
Dia. 2¹/16 in. (5.3 cm)
On loan to Middlebury College Museum of Art

Alexander III took part in the ceremony to lay
the keel of the imperial yacht *Polar Star* in
1888. Two years later it was launched. Nikolai
Nabokov provided drawings for the interiors,
which were created by the furniture firm of
Svirskii. While the Imperial Glassworks created a large service of glassware for the yacht,
decorated with an engraved double-headed
eagle, a matching set of porcelain was never
made.

33. Tea set

St. Petersburg, 1894
Firm of the Brothers Grachëv
Silver, gilding, ivory

cat. 33

Teapot: H. 6¾ in. (17.2 cm), W. 8½ in.
(21.6 cm), D. 6³/8 in. (16.2 cm)
Hot water pot: H. 6⁵/8 in (16.8 cm), W. 8¾ in.
(22.2 cm), D. 5⁷/16 in. (13.8 cm)
Creamer: H. 3³/8 in. (8.6 cm), W. 6½ in.
(16.5 cm), D. 4½ in. (11.5 cm)
Sugar: H. 4⁷/16 in. (11.3 cm), W. 7½ in.
(19.1 cm), D. 5⁵/8 in. (14.3 cm)
Middlebury College Museum of Art, Gift of
Nancy and Edward Wynkoop, 2001.020.1–.4

Marks: crossed anchors; *A Sh* in Cyrillic for an
unknown assayer; *1894*; *84*; *Grachëv* in Cyrillic
with imperial warrant; the mark of the assayer
is missing from one of the pots

Decorated with the monogram *GM* and an
imperial crown, this tea set (with its tray
below) was made for Grand Duke Georgii
Mikhailovich.

34. Tray

St. Petersburg, 1894
Firm of the Brothers Grachëv
Silver
L. 25⁷/8 in. (65.7 cm), W. 15¹/8 in. (38.4 cm)
Middlebury College Museum of Art,
2001.020.6

Marks: *A Sh* in Cyrillic for an unknown assayer; *1894*; *84*; *Grachëv* in Cyrillic with imperial
warrant

Engraved *GM* in Cyrillic under an imperial
crown for Georgii Mikhailovich
Engraved on the bottom: *v.5f .71z* (weight
measurement, standing for *ves 5 funt 71
zolotnik*)

35. Part of a service of flatware

St. Petersburg, 1894 and ca. 1909
Firm of the Brothers Grachëv
Silver, except for knife blade; gilding on gravy
ladle, lemon fork, salt spoon, and tea strainer
Dinner knife: L. 11¼ in. (28.6 cm); marks:
crossed anchors; 84; on blade: *Varypaev* in
Cyrillic with imperial warrant
Dinner fork: L. 8½ in. (21.6 cm); marks:
crossed anchors; *AS* in Cyrillic for assayer
Aleksandr Sev'er; *1894*; *84*; *Br. Grachëv* in
Cyrillic with imperial warrant
Soup spoon: L. 9¹⁵/₁₆ in. (25.2 cm); marks:
crossed anchors; *I E* in Cyrillic for an unknown assayer; *1886*; *84*; *Grachëv* in Cyrillic;
KR in Cyrillic for an unknown workmaster
Dessert knife: L. 8½ in. (21.6 cm); marks:
kokoshnik facing right; alpha for St. Petersburg; *84*; *Br. Grachëv* in Cyrillic with imperial
warrant
Dessert fork: L. 7 in. (17.8 cm); marks:
kokoshnik facing right; alpha for St. Petersburg; *84*; *Br Grachëv* in Cyrillic with imperial
warrant
Dessert spoon: L. 7³/₁₆ in. (18.3 cm); marks:
kokoshnik facing right; alpha for St. Petersburg; *84*; *Br Grachëv* in Cyrillic with imperial
warrant
Teaspoon: L. 6¹/₁₆ in. (15.4 cm); marks:
crossed anchors; *AS* in Cyrillic for assayer
Aleksandr Sev'er; *1894*; *84*; *Grachëv* in Cyrillic
with imperial warrant
Gravy ladle: L. 7¼ in. (18.4 cm); marks:
crossed anchors; *84*; *Grachëv* in Cyrillic
Lemon fork: L. 4¹⁵/₁₆ in. (12.6 cm); marks:
crossed anchors; *84*; *Grachëv* in Cyrillic with
imperial warrant
Salt spoon: L. 4⁷/₁₆ in. (11.3 cm); marks:
kokoshnik facing right; alpha for St. Petersburg; *84*; *Br Grachëv* in Cyrillic with imperial
warrant
Tea strainer: L. 6⁷/₁₆ in. (16.4 cm); marks:
crossed anchors; *AF* in Cyrillic for an unknown assayer; *1883*; *84*; *Grachëv* in Cyrillic;
G[?] O in Cyrillic for an unknown workmaster. Tea strainer handle has been attached
to an older tea strainer.
Salt cellar: L. 3¹⁵/₁₆ in. (10 cm), W. 3 in. (7.6
cm); marks: crossed anchors; *AS* in Cyrillic
for assayer Aleksandr Sever; *1894*; *84*; *Grachëv*
in Cyrillic with imperial warrant

All pieces are engraved *GM* in Cyrillic, the
monogram of Georgii Mikhailovich, under the
imperial crown.

On loan to Middlebury College Museum of
Art, L 121.1993

It is not unusual to find different dates and
often the marks of different makers on sets of
silverware. Various firms produced the soup
spoons in this set. Judging by marks on the
pieces, a dessert service was added to the dinner flatware sometime after 1908 and before
1914. This silver service, including the tea set,
was kept at Harax, the Crimean estate of
Georgii Mikhailovich. Those who escaped Russia with the Dowager Empress in 1919
brought it with them.

36. Dinner fork and soup spoon

St. Petersburg, 1857
Nichols and Plinke
Silver
Fork: L. 8⅜ in. (21.3 cm)
Spoon: L. 9¹⁵/₁₆ in. (25.2 cm)
On loan to Middlebury College Museum of
Art, L 121.1993

Marks: crossed anchors; *AM* in Cyrillic for assayer Aleksandr Mitin; *1857*; *84*; *N P* for Nichols
and Plinke; *PK* for an unknown workmaster;
soup spoon has *EB* in Cyrillic for assayer
Eduard Brandenberg

Both are engraved with *MN* in Cyrillic, the
monogram of Mikhail Nikolaevich, under the
imperial crown

A note accompanying the fork and spoon says
that they were the only two pieces Grand
Duchess Maria Georgievna was able to preserve
of the silver that once belonged to her father-
in-law, Grand Duke Mikhail Nikolaevich.

37. Pair of candlesticks

Moscow, 1887–96
Firm of Fabergé
Silver
Each H. 10¾ in. (27.3 cm)
Hillwood Museum and Gardens, 12.156.1–.2

Marks: St. George and dragon; *84*; *Fabergé* in
Cyrillic with imperial warrant; inventory
number *10583*

These candlesticks came with a card saying they had belonged to Grand Duke Aleksei Aleksandrovich, an uncle of Nicholas II (unverified). The grand duke made a celebrated six-week trip to the United States in 1871. He visited New York, Philadelphia, and Boston before he went on to the Midwest and saw Chicago, Cleveland, Detroit, and St. Louis. At the end of his official trip he spent several weeks traveling in the West, meeting General George Custer and William F. "Buffalo Bill" Cody, and shooting buffalo. He ended his trip with Mardi Gras in New Orleans.

38. Desk set

St. Petersburg, 1908–17
Firm of Fabergé
Henrik Wigström (1862–1923), workmaster
Birch, silver gilt, enamel

Stationery holder (12.147.1): H. 7 in. (17.8 cm), W. 8¾ in. (21.4 cm)
Tray, inkwell, gum pot, sand box (12.147.2): overall H. 3¹⁵/₁₆ in. (10 cm), W. 9¼ in (23.5 cm), D. 5¾ in. (14.6 cm)
Blotter holder (12.147.3): L. 5³/₁₆ in. (13.2 cm)
Note pad (12.147.4): H. 6 in. (15.3 cm), W. 4⅞ in. (11.2 cm)
Letter opener (12.147.5): L. 11¼ in. (25.8 cm)
Pen (12.147.6): L. 7½ in. (19 cm)
Hillwood Museum and Gardens

Marks: the most complete marks are on the metal inserts for the inkwell, gum pot, and sand box: kokoshnik facing right; alpha for St. Petersburg; 88; Fabergé in Latin letters; HW for Henrik Wigström; inventory number 23058; an unidentified import mark; 925 for silver standard; r for London 1912 on the stationery holder

39. Pen rest

St. Petersburg, before 1896
Firm of Fabergé
Anders Nevaleinen (1858–1933), workmaster
Silver, bowenite
H. ¹⁵/₁₆ in. (2.4 cm), W. 2⅞ in. (6.1 cm), D. 1¹/₆ in. (2.7 cm)
On loan to Middlebury College Museum of Art, L 68.1993

Marks: crossed anchors; AN for Anders Nevaleinen; scratch number 58954

40. Bear paperweight

Russia, late 19th–early 20th century
Bronze, gilding
H. 1⅞ in. (4.8 cm), W. 6½ in. (16.6 cm), D. 2¾ in. (7 cm)
On loan to Middlebury College Museum of Art, L 86.1993

41. Paperweight

St. Petersburg, ca. 1900
Nephrite, chalcedony, gold, enamel
L. 2¾ in. (7 cm), W. 2⅜ in. (6.1 cm)
On loan to Middlebury College Museum of Art, L 61.1993

A cameo portrait of Alexandra Fedorovna after a design by Augustus K. Timus (b. 1865) is set into the nephrite.

42. Letter opener

Russia, late 19th–early 20th century
Ivory
L. 10⅞ in. (27.7 cm), W. 1¼ in. (3.2 cm)
On loan to Middlebury College Museum of Art, L 109.1993

The letter opener is decorated with the coat of arms of imperial Russia.

43. Reading clip

St. Petersburg, before 1896
Gold, sapphires
H. 2¾ in. (7 cm), W. ⅞ in. (2.3 cm)
On loan to Middlebury College Museum of Art, L 75.1993

Marks: crossed anchors; 56; BF in Cyrillic for unidentified maker

Grand Duchess Kseniia, sister of Nicholas II, presented this as a gift to Nancy Wynkoop, its present owner and her distant cousin.

44. Seal

St. Petersburg, ca. 1900
Firm of Fabergé
Gold, nephrite, enamel, diamonds
H. 1⅝ in. (3.8 cm), Dia. ⅞ in. (2.3 cm)
On loan to Middlebury College Museum of Art, L 66.1993

Marks: inventory number 5820

The seal itself is an imperial crown.

45. Bowl

St. Petersburg, early 20th century
Silver gilt, bowenite, ruby
H. 2½ in. (6.4 cm), Dia. 2⅜ in. (6.1 cm)
Middlebury College Museum of Art, Gift of
Nancy and Edward Wynkoop, 2000.039

The mounts of the bowl, like those on the
presentation dish awarded after the signing of
the Treaty of Portsmouth, are in the form of
serpents, a favorite motif of the Fabergé firm.

46. Tapir

St. Petersburg, ca. 1900
Firm of Fabergé
Obsidian, gold, rubies
H. 2⅜ in. (6.1 cm), W. 3⅞ in. (9.9 cm), D. 1⅜
in. (3.5 cm)
Middlebury College Museum of Art, Gift of
Nancy and Edward Wynkoop, 1999.020

Grand Duke Georgii Mikhailovich or his
brother Sergei commissioned this tapir with a
pince-nez as a joke for Maria Georgievna, who
was very nearsighted. Her brother-in-law
Sergei teased her that she reminded him of a
tapir wearing a pince-nez.

47. Tweedledum

St. Petersburg, 1907–14
Firm of Fabergé
Obsidian, bowenite, rhodonite, lapis lazuli,
demantoid garnet
H. 2 in. (5.1 cm), W. 1³/₁₆ in. (3.1 cm),
D. ⅞ in. (2.3 cm)
On loan to Middlebury College Museum of
Art, L 78.1993

Only one other figure of Tweedledum is
known. It is carved together with Tweedledee
in the Thai Royal Collection.

48. Figure of a "Chinaman"

St. Petersburg, 1907–14
Firm of Fabergé
Obsidian, jade, purpurite, agate, lapis lazuli,
diamonds
H. 1⅞ in. (4.8 cm), W. 1⁷/₁₆ in. (3.7 cm),
D. ⅞ in. (2.3 cm)
On loan to Middlebury College Museum of
Art, L 79.1993

These composites of different hardstones are
among the smallest figures that Fabergé
made. This is the only known figure of a
"Chinaman."

49. Cigarette box

St. Petersburg, 1903
Firm of Fabergé
Henrik Wigström (1862–1923), workmaster
Silver, gold, silk cord, coin
H. 4¼ in. (10.8 cm), W. 2⁷/₁₆ in. (6.2 cm),
D. ⅞ in. (2.3 cm)
On loan to Middlebury College Museum of
Art, L 83.1993

Marks: *88*; *Fabergé* in Cyrillic; *HW* for Henrik
Wigström

Engraved: *Kseniia 9 April 1903* and inside *From
Tommy 1921*

50. Cigarette box

St. Petersburg, ca. 1890
Firm of Karl Hahn (Gan)
Gun metal, gold, ruby, silk cord
H. 3¹³/₁₆ in. (9.7 cm), W. 2¾ in. (7 cm),
D. ¹³/₁₆ in. (2.1 cm)
On loan to Middlebury College Museum of
Art, L 84.1993

Applied cipher *GM* in Cyrillic for Grand Duke
Georgii Mikhailovich and inscription in Russian: *1 priz' za igru lawn tennis / Henry Harrison /
Georgii* (First prize for the game of lawn tennis)
along with *Cannes March 5/17 1890*

The cigarette box came in its own box marked
in Cyrillic *K. Gan /Nevsk. prosp. No 26 / S.P. Burg*

This box came with a card from Mrs. Leland
Harrison, who was apparently giving the box
back to Georgii's family.

51. Ashtray

St. Petersburg, ca. 1913
Firm of Karl Hahn (Gan)
Silver
H. 4⅝ in. (11.7 cm), W. 4⅝ in. (11.7 cm)
Hillwood Museum and Gardens, 12.163

Marks: kokoshnik facing right; alpha for St. Petersburg; *88*; *K. Gan* in Cyrillic for Karl Gan
(Hahn) with imperial warrant

Decorated with the Cap of Monomakh above the double-headed eagle instead of the imperial crown, this ashtray must have been a souvenir of the Tercentenary. It was said to have come from the study of Nicholas II at the Alexander Palace at Tsarskoe Selo (unverified).

52. Frame

Russia, 1880s
Gilded brass, photograph
H. 4⅞ in. (12.4 cm), W. 2⅞ in. (7.4 cm)
On loan to Middlebury College Museum of Art, L 106.1993

Photograph of Alexander III and his wife Maria Fedorovna

53. Frame

St. Petersburg, 1903–1908; miniature, London
Firm of Fabergé
Henrik Wigström (1862–1923), workmaster; Neydemann, miniaturist
Gold, enamel, miniature on ivory
H. 4⁵/₁₆ in. (11 cm), W. 3 in. (7.7 cm)
Middlebury College Museum of Art, Gift of Nancy and Edward Wynkoop, 1993.018

Marks: kokoshnik facing left; *56*; *Fabergé* in Cyrillic; *HW* for Henrik Wigström

Signed: *Neydemann London*

Miniature of Alexander III and Maria Georgievna

cat. 53

54. Tenth Anniversary frame

St. Petersburg, ca. 1910
Firm of Fabergé
Hjalmar Armfelt (1873–1959), workmaster
Coppered silver, miniatures on ivory
H. 7½ in. (19.1 cm), W. 6 in. (15.3 cm)
Middlebury College Museum of Art, Gift of Nancy and Edward Wynkoop, 2001.022

Marks: kokoshnik facing right; *88*; *Ia A* in Cyrillic for Hjalmar Armfelt; on stand *Fabergé* in Cyrillic

On front the dates: *1900 / 1910 / 30 / IV*

Grand Duke Georgii Mikhailovich and Maria Georgievna married on 30 April 1900. This tenth anniversary frame includes miniatures of Georgii and his two daughters, Princess Nina and Princess Xenia.

55. Triptych frame

St. Petersburg, ca. 1908
Firm of Fabergé
Viktor Aarne (1863–1934), workmaster
Gold, enamel, pearls, diamond, miniatures on ivory
H. 3⅜ in. (8.6 cm), W. 4⅛ in. (10.5 cm)
Middlebury College Museum of Art, Gift of Nancy and Edward Wynkoop, 2000.038

Marks: kokoshnik facing left for 1896–1908; unclear assayer mark; *56* for gold standard; *Fabergé* in Cyrillic; *VA* in Cyrillic for Viktor Aarne; inventory number *2518*

Miniatures of Princesses Xenia and Nina flank one of their mother, Grand Duchess Maria Georgievna.

The translucent blue enamel covers a guilloché, or machine engraved, surface and allows the pattern to show through. Red enamel is mixed with brown to simulate wood.

56. Diptych frame

St. Petersburg, ca. 1908
Firm of Fabergé
Viktor Aarne (1863–1934), workmaster
Gold, enamel, diamonds, ivory, photographs
H. 4½ in. (11.4 cm), W. 4⅜ in. (11.2 cm)
On loan to Middlebury College Museum of Art, L 58.1993

Marks: *kokoshnik* facing left; *Ia L* in Cyrillic for assayer Iakov Lapunov; *88*; *Fabergé* in Cyrillic; *VA* in Cyrillic for Viktor Aarne

Photographs of Grand Duke Georgii Mikhailovich, Grand Duchess Maria Georgievna, their daughter, Princess Nina, and her niece, Nancy Wynkoop, are inserted into the openings.

57. Circular frame

Moscow, ca. 1904
Firm of Fabergé
Gold, enamel, ivory, photograph
Dia. 2⅛ in. (5.4 cm)
On loan to Middlebury College Museum of Art, L 62.1993

Marks: *kokoshnik* facing left; *IL* in Cyrillic for Moscow assayer Ivan Lebedkin; *56*; *KF* in Cyrillic for Karl Fabergé; inventory number *25538*

Photograph of Princess Xenia

58. Star-shaped frame

St. Petersburg, ca. 1904
Firm of Fabergé
Viktor Aarne (1863–1934), workmaster
Silver gilt, enamel, pearls, ivory, photograph
H. 2⁵/₁₆ in. (5.9 cm), W. 2⁵/₁₆ in. (5.9 cm)
On loan to Middlebury College Museum of Art, L 63.1993

Marks: *88*; *Fabergé* in Cyrillic; *VA* in Cyrillic for Viktor Aarne; inventory number *2411*

Photograph of Grand Duke Georgii Mikhailovich

59. Frame

St. Petersburg, ca. 1896
Firm of Fabergé
Mikhail Perkhin (1860–1903), workmaster
Silver gilt, nephrite, photograph with applied watercolor
Dia. 1½ in. (3.8 cm)
Middlebury College Museum of Art, Gift of Nancy and Edward Wynkoop, 1993.019

Marks: St. George and the dragon; *84*; *MP* in Cyrillic for Mikhail Perkhin

Photograph of Grand Duchess Maria Georgievna

60. Wooden diptych frame

St. Petersburg, ca. 1906
Firm of Fabergé
Anders Nevaleinen (1858–1933), workmaster
Silver gilt, wood
H. 4⅞ in. (12.4 cm), W. 5⅞ in. (15 cm)
On loan to Middlebury College Museum of Art, L 92.1993

Marks: *kokoshnik* facing left; *AR* in Cyrillic for St. Petersburg assayer A. Rikhter; *88*; *AN* in Cyrillic for Anders Nevaleinen; inventory number *13597*

Photographs of Princesses Nina and Xenia

61. Frame

St. Petersburg, ca. 1904
Firm of Fabergé
Henrik Wigström (1862–1923), workmaster
Gold, nephrite, enamel, photograph
H. 7¹/₁₆ in. (17.9 cm), W. 5¹¹/₁₆ in. (14.5 cm)
On loan to Middlebury College Museum of Art, L 60.1993

Marks: *kokoshnik* facing left; *AR* in Cyrillic for assayer A. Rikhter; *56*; *Fabergé* in Cyrillic; *HW* for Henrik Wigström

Later photograph of Princess Helen of Greece, niece of Maria Georgievna

62. Two frames

Paris, ca. 1910
Firm of Cartier
Gold, silver, enamel, ivory, photographs
Each Dia. 2 in. (5.1 cm)
Hillwood Museum and Gardens, 11.54.1–.2

Mark: *Cartier*

Photographs of Nicholas II's two oldest daughters—Grand Duchess Olga is in the green frame and Grand Duchess Tatiana is in the salmon one—are seen here. These frames reveal how Cartier copied Fabergé's style in order to compete with him more successfully. They are said to have come from the private apartments of Nicholas and Alexandra at Tsarskoe Selo (unverified).

63. Ice pendant

St. Petersburg, ca. 1910
Firm of Fabergé

Albert Holmström (1876–1925), workmaster
Alma Phil (1888–1976), designer
Rock crystal, diamonds, platinum
H. 2½ in. (6.4 cm), W. 1 in. (2.6 cm),
D.½ in. (1.3 cm)
Middlebury College Museum of Art, Gift of
Nancy and Edward Wynkoop, 2001.021

Dr. Emanuel Nobel, the oil tycoon and
nephew of Alfred Nobel (the inventor of dyna-
mite and after whom the Nobel Prize is
named), was famous for his extravagant parties. For one dinner he ordered an ice pendant
as a souvenir of the evening for each lady who
attended. Alma Phil also designed and then
created with her uncle, Albert Holmström, the
1913 Winter Egg, a gift from Nicholas II to his
mother, Maria Fedorovna.

According to the donor, Georgii Mikhailovich
gave this pendant to Princess Helen of Greece,
who in turn presented it to Princess Xenia.

64. Charm bracelet

St. Petersburg, ca. 1910
Gold, silver, enamel, diamonds, rubies, pearl,
various semiprecious stones
Open: L. 7¾ in. (19.7 cm)
On loan to Middlebury College Museum of
Art, L 95.1993

This bracelet includes eggs, one possibly by
Fabergé, of the type women received as gifts at
Easter and then attached to a necklace or
bracelet. Among the other charms are one
with the monogram GM set in diamonds and
rubies and two replicas of crowns.

65. Three miniature eggs

St. Petersburg, late 19th–early 20th century
Yellow (L 80.1993.1): gold, enamel; H. 13/16 in.
   (2.1 cm), W.½ in. (1.3 cm); mark: 56
Orange (L 80.1993.2): chalcedony, diamonds;
   H. ¾ in. (2 cm), W. ⅜ in. (1 cm)
White (L 80.1993.3): gold, enamel; H. ⅞ in.
   (2.3 cm), W. ½ in. (1.3 cm); mark: 56
On loan to Middlebury College Museum of Art

Husbands gave their wives and daughters this
type of egg at Easter. Women collected them
and attached them to a necklace or bracelet
that they then wore for forty days after Easter.
See also the charm bracelet above.

66. Red miniature egg

St. Petersburg, before 1896
Firm of Fabergé
Mikhail Perkhin (1860–1903), workmaster
Gold, enamel, opal
H. ⅞ in. (2.3 cm), W. ½ in. (1.3 cm)
On loan to Middlebury College Museum of
Art, L 81.1993

Marks: crossed anchors; 56; MP in Cyrillic for
Mikhail Perkhin

67. Kite-shaped locket

St. Petersburg, ca. 1910
Silver, enamel, diamond
H. 1⅛ in. (2.9 cm), W. ⅝ in. (1.6 cm)
On loan to Middlebury College Museum of
Art, L 127.1993

Marks: 88; FA in Cyrillic for an unknown
maker

Inscription in Russian: From great-grandmother
A.J. 1910

Alexandra Iosifovna (Josifovna), whose initials
appear on this locket, was the wife of Konstantin Nikolaevich and the great-grandmother of
Xenia, the daughter of Grand Duke Georgii.

68. Blue enamel locket

St. Petersburg, ca. 1900
Firm of Ivan Britsyn
Silver gilt, enamel, photograph
Dia. 1¼ in. (3.2 cm)
On loan to Middlebury College Museum of
Art, L 65.1993.1

Marks: 88; IB in Cyrillic for Ivan Britsyn

A photograph of Grand Duke Mikhail Nikolaevich, father of Georgii Mikhailovich, is inside the locket.

69. White enamel locket

St. Petersburg, ca. 1900
Silver gilt, enamel, photograph
Dia. 1¼ in. (3.2 cm)
On loan to Middlebury College Museum of
Art, L 65.1993.2

Contains a photograph of Georgii
Mikhailovich

70. Pink enamel locket

St. Petersburg, ca. 1900
Silver gilt, enamel, diamonds, photographs
Dia. 1 in. (2.6 cm)
On loan to Middlebury College Museum of
Art, L 65.1993.3

Holds two photographs of unidentified babies

71. Ring box

St. Petersburg, early 20th century
Holly wood, glass, gold, velvet
H. 1¹³/₁₆ in. (4.7 cm), W. 7 in. (17.8 cm), D. 3⅝
in. (9.3 cm)
On loan to Middlebury College Museum of
Art, L 96.1993

The monogram of Grand Duchess Maria
Georgievna is engraved on a glass panel inset
in the lid.

72. Triptych icon

Moscow, before 1896
Firm of Ivan Khlebnikov
Silver, enamel
Closed: H. 5 in. (12.8 cm), W. 3 in. (7.7 cm)
On loan to Middlebury College Museum of
Art, L 73.1993

Marks: St. George and the dragon; *84*; *I Khlebnikov* with imperial warrant

The icon depicts the Kazan Mother of God
with two saints, Saint George and an unidentified female saint. The painting is quite worn.

73. Icon, Iverskaia Mother of God

Moscow, 1896–1908
Firm of Ovchinnikov
Tempera on wood, silver gilt, enamel, seed
pearls, velvet
H. 4¾ in. (12.1 cm), W. 4⁵/₁₆ in. (11 cm)
Hillwood Museum and Gardens, 54.30

Marks: kokoshnik facing left; *IL* in Cyrillic for
Moscow assayer Ivan Lebedkin; *84*; *P. Ovchinnikov* in Cyrillic with imperial warrant

This icon was said to have come from the
Alexander Palace (unverified).

74. Icon of Christ Emmanuel

Moscow, 1908–17
Firm of Ivan Khlebnikov

Silver gilt, tempera on wood, silk brocade
H. 3⅛ in. (8 cm), W. 2⅜ in. (6.1 cm)
On loan to Middlebury College Museum of
Art, L 101.1993

Marks: kokoshnik facing right; delta for
Moscow; *84*; *I Kh* in Cyrillic for Ivan
Khlebnikov

75. Icon of the Kazan Mother of God

Moscow, 1908–17
Firm of Ivan Khlebnikov
Sergei Vashkov (1879–1914), designer
Silver gilt, tempera on wood, emeralds, aqua-
marines, tourmaline, amethyst, silk brocade
H. 3⁹/₁₆ in. (8.9 cm), W. 4½ in. (11.7 cm)

cat. 75

Fig. 40. Icon of the Korsun Mother of God. From Sergei
Vashkov, *Religiosnoe iskusstvo* (Religious Art), 1911. Hillwood Museum and Gardens Art Library.

On loan to Middlebury College Museum of Art, L 70.1993

Marks: kokoshnik facing right; delta for Moscow; *84*; possible *I Kh* for Ivan Khlebnikov

In this three-part icon, two archangels, Michael and Gabriel, flank the Kazan Mother of God. Since an almost identical icon appears in a collection of Vashkov's designs for the firm of Olovianishnikov (see fig. 40), it appears that he designed for other firms as well.

76. Icon of Metropolitan Aleksei

Moscow, 1899–1906
Tempera on wood, silver, enamel, fabric, brass plaque
H. 10⁹/16 in. (26.8 cm), W. 8¹³/16 (22.4 cm)
Hillwood Museum and Gardens, 54.26

Marks on oklad: kokoshnik facing left; *IL* in Cyrillic for Moscow assayer Ivan Lebedkin; *84*; *AS* in Cyrillic for an unknown maker

Inscription on brass plaque on the back in Russian: *To our dear Godchild His Imperial Highness the Tsarevich Grand Duke Aleksei Nikolaevich from the Reservists of the Starorusskii District who came back from the Far East 1906*

Nicholas II named his son after Tsar Aleksei Mikhailovich, the father of Peter the Great. Saint Aleksei, who served as Metropolitan of

Moscow from 1354 to 1378, was the patron saint of both Aleksei Mikhailovich and Tsarevich Aleksei. Because the tsarevich was born during the Russo-Japanese War, Nicholas II declared that all soldiers then serving in the military were godfathers to the heir to the imperial throne.

77. Icon, Mother of God, "Surety of Sinners"

St. Petersburg, early 20th century
Tempera on wood, gold, diamonds, emeralds, pearls, brass plaque
H. 5 in. (12.7 cm), W. 3¹³/16 in. (9.7 cm)
Hillwood Museum and Gardens, 54.27

Inscription on four banderoles on oklad in Russian: *I am the guarantor for sinners before my son / That they who bring their joy to me always / Through me ask for eternal joy*

Inscription on plaque on the back in Russian: *To His Imperial Highness the Tsarevich and Grand Duke Aleksei Nikolaevich with the blessings of the Convent of St. John (First Class) in St. Petersburg as a token of incessant prayerful memory. 22 August 1912*

In 1912 Tsarevich Alexis suffered a severe attack of hemophilia, and it was thought he would not survive. This icon was among the many he received at that time wishing him well.

78. Easter egg

St. Petersburg, 1885–1917
Imperial Porcelain Factory
Hard-paste porcelain, gilding
H. 3½ in. (8.9 cm), Dia. 2⅞ in. (7.4 cm)
On loan to Middlebury College Museum of Art, L 90.1993

Stenciled monogram *MF* in Cyrillic for Maria Fedorovna

Each year at Easter the emperors and empresses presented to members of the court porcelain eggs such as these and the two following. Alexander III and his wife Maria Fedorovna started giving eggs decorated with their ciphers in the mid-1880s.

cat. 76

79. Two porcelain Easter eggs

St. Petersburg, 1894–1917
Imperial Porcelain Factory
Hard-paste porcelain
White egg with monogram *AF* in Cyrillic for
Alexandra Fedorovna (25.387): H. 4⁵/₁₆ in.
(11 cm), W. 3½ in. (8.9 cm)
Blue egg with monogram *N II* in Cyrillic for
Nicholas II (25.385): H. 3³/₈ in. (8.6 cm),
W. 2⁹/₁₆ in. (6.5 cm)
Hillwood Museum and Gardens

80. Easter egg with painting of Saint
Dmitrii

St. Petersburg, 1890s
Imperial Porcelain Factory
Osip Chirikov (d. 1903), designer
Hard-paste porcelain
H. 4½ in. (11.4 cm)
Hillwood Museum and Gardens, 25.390

Inscription on front in Russian: *Holy Pious
Tsarevich Dmitrii*

Alexander III turned to the icon painter Osip
Chirikov in 1887 for drawings of Easter eggs
depicting eighteen saints and twelve feasts. The
Moscow architect Aleksandr Kaminskii provided the designs for the Russian-style cross on
the back. Tsarevich Dmitrii, son of Ivan the
Terrible, the last Riurik tsar, was believed to
have been killed on the orders of Boris Godunov in 1591.

81. Double-sided panagia

Russia, 19th century
Gilded silver, tempera on wood
H. 3½ in. (9 cm)
On loan to Middlebury College Museum of
Art, L 72.1993

Inscription in Russian: *The depiction of the
miracle-working Mother of God of Akhtyrka, who
appeared in the year 1739, the 2nd day of June*
Part of the inscription is covered with a tiny
plaque of a double-headed eagle, although the
inscription and the double-headed eagle regularly appear on icons of the Akhtyrka Mother
of God

On the other side in Russian: *?? the New and
the Blesser of Nikita* (the inscriptions are badly
worn)

The Akhtyrka Mother of God is depicted on
one side and what appear to be Saints Helari-
on the New, Abbott of Pelecete, and Nikita,
Bishop of Novgorod, on the other.

82. Panagia

Moscow, 1908–17
Firm of Olovianishnikov and Sons
Sergei Vashkov (1879–1914), designer
Silver gilt, aquamarines, peridots, amethysts,
sapphires, mother-of-pearl
H. 4 in. (10.2 cm), W. 2⁵/₈ in. (6.7 cm)
On loan to Middlebury College Museum of
Art, L 71.1993

Marks: kokoshnik facing right; *84; O. Sei* in
Cyrillic for Olovianishnikov and Sons; on
hanger *AMP* or *AMB* in Cyrillic for an unknown maker

Inscription in Russian: *Rejoice, the star revealing
the sun*

A panagia, worn by an Eastern Orthodox arch-
bishop, usually includes the image of the
Mother of God. Here, the Vladimir Mother of
God is painted on mother-of-pearl. Sergei
Vashkov, chief designer for the firm of Olo-
vianishnikov and Sons, designed this piece.
The firm was the premier producer of ecclesi-
astical art in the neo-Russian and neo-
Byzantine style.

83. Chalice

Moscow, ca. 1914
Firm of Olovianishnikov and Sons
Sergei Vashkov (1879–1914), designer
Silver, glass, enamel, ivory, semiprecious stones
H. 7½ in. (19.1 cm), Dia. 5³/₈ in. (13.6 cm)
Hillwood Museum and Gardens, 12.614
Museum purchase 1993

Marks: kokoshnik facing right; delta for
Moscow; *84; Tvo O. Sei* in Cyrillic for Con-
glomerate Olovianishnikov and Sons

Inscription in Greek: *For this is my blood / Drink
of it, all of you*

This chalice was part of a liturgical set made
for a cave chapel in the basement of the Court
Hospital in Tsarskoe Selo. Court architect Silvio Danini designed the chapel in the neo-
Byzantine style, and Vashkov designed the
liturgical set, which included this chalice, in
the same style.

84. A Boyar Wedding Feast

Munich, late 1880s
Brukman (photographer), copy of a painting
by Konstantin E. Makovskii (1839–1915)
Photogravure
H. 22⅜ in. (56.8 cm), W. 34½ in. (87.6 cm)
Hillwood Museum and Gardens, 56.36
Museum purchase 1999

Stamped in English on the print: COPYRIGHT
1885 / BY / Chas. W. Schumann; printed in Russian: Edition and Property of M.D. Volf and Co.;
in Russian: Photograph Brukman in Munich; in
English: Copyright 1885 by C.W. Schumann / For
sale by Geo. Kirchner & Co., N.Y.

Konstantin Makovskii painted A Boyar Wedding
Feast, now at Hillwood Museum, in 1883. Two
years later he exhibited it in Antwerp, where
Charles W. Schumann, an American jewelry
merchant, purchased it. Schumann exhibited
the painting in his New York jewelry shop on
Broadway. He had photographs and chromo-
lithographs made, which he copyrighted for
widespread distribution. Through these media
the painting became extremely popular in the
United States. The painting fully expresses the
romantic view that many late nineteenth-
century Russians had of seventeenth-century
boyar life.

85. Part of a tea set

Moscow, 1899–1908
Firm of Gustav Klingert
Silver gilt, enamel
Teapot (15.112.1) H. 4¾ in. (12.1 cm), W. 8 in.
(20.3 cm)
Creamer (15.112.2) H. 3⁹/₁₆ in. (9 cm)
Sugar (15.112.3) H. 3 in. (7.6 cm)
Hillwood Museum and Gardens

Marks: kokoshnik facing left; IL in Cyrillic for
Moscow assayer Ivan Lebedkin; 84; GK in
Cyrillic for Gustav Klingert

This type of filigree enamel was the most common type produced by the Moscow silversmiths and was sold widely in the United
States. Klingert exhibited his works in the
World's Columbian Exposition in Chicago in
1893, where he won a bronze medal. His initials appear occasionally with "Tiffany & Co."

86. Tea glass holder and glass

Moscow, 1888
Firm of Ovchinnikov
Silver gilt, enamel, glass
H. 3¹³/₁₆ in. (9.7 cm), W. 4½ in. (11.4 cm)
Hillwood Museum and Gardens, 15.41

Marks: St. George and the dragon; VS in Cyrillic for Moscow assayer Viktor Savinkov; 1888;
88; Ovchinnikov in Cyrillic with imperial
warrant

Men usually drank their tea in glasses, while
women sipped theirs from cups and saucers.
This tea glass holder and glass came from the
collection of Queen Olga of Greece, mother of
Grand Duchess Maria Georgievna, and her son
Prince Christopher of Greece, who was Maria's
brother.

87. Lacquered spoon

Moscow, late 19th century
Firm of Mariia Semenova
Silver, enamel
H. 4¼ in. (10.8 cm), W. ⅞ in. (2.3 cm)
On loan to Middlebury College Museum of
Art, L 107.1993

Marks: MS in Cyrillic for Mariia Semenova

88. Champlevé enameled spoon

Moscow, 1875
Firm of Ovchinnikov
Silver gilt, enamel
H. 7⅛ in. (18.1 cm), W. 2⅜ in. (6.1 cm)
On loan to Middlebury College Museum of
Art, L 88.1993

Marks: IK in Cyrillic for an unknown assayer;
1875; 91; PO in Cyrillic for Pavel Ovchinnikov

89. Spoon with view of the Kremlin

Moscow, before 1896
Firm of Vasilii Semenov
Silver, niello
H. 7 in. (17.8 cm), W. 2½ in. (6.4 cm)
On loan to Middlebury College Museum of
Art, L 89.1993

Marks: St. George and the dragon; IK in Cyrillic for an unknown assayer; illegible date; 84;
VS in Cyrillic for Vasilii Semenov

Vasilii Semenov was one of the most prolific producers of Russian niello wares. Following his death in 1896, his daughter Mariia took over his firm (see cat. 87).

90. Vodka cup

Moscow, late 19th century
Attributed to Firm of Ovchinnikov
Silver, enamel
H. 3⅛ in. (7.9 cm), Dia. 1¹¹/₁₆ in. (4.3 cm)
On loan to Middlebury College Museum of Art, L 87.1993

The vodka cup is executed in the technique of plique-à-jour enamel, where no backing appears behind the enamel. Pavel Ovchinnikov perfected this technique in the late nineteenth century.

91. Cup and saucer

Moscow, 1893
Firm of Antip Kuzmichev, made for Tiffany & Co.
Silver gilt, enamel
Cup: Dia. 3¼ in. (8.4 cm)
Saucer: Dia. 5¼ in. (13.4 cm)
Private collection

Marks: St. George and the dragon; *LO* in Cyrillic for Moscow assayer Lev Fleks; *1893*; *88*; *AK* in Cyrillic for Antip Kuzmichev; in English: *Made for Tiffany & Co.*

Monogram on saucer: monogram ETW engraved on saucer

Kuzmichev sold enamels through Tiffany & Co. in the late nineteenth and early twentieth centuries. This cup and saucer is in plique-à-jour enamel. Such objects were not really intended for use. The initials *ETW* in Latin letters were probably engraved on the saucer at Tiffany for the customer.

92. Kovsh

Moscow, 1896
Firm of Antip Kuzmichev, made for Tiffany & Co.
Silver gilt, enamel
H. ⁷/₁₆ in. (1.1 cm), L. 3¾ in. (9.5 cm),
Dia. of bowl 2 in. (5 cm)
Private collection

Marks: St. George and the dragon; *LO* in Cyrillic for Moscow assayer Lev Oleks; *1896*; *88*; *AK* in Cyrillic for Antip Kuzmichev; in English: *Made for Tiffany & Co.*

Monogram *MC* engraved in English on underside of handle

93. Kovsh

Moscow, 1908–17
Firm of Ivan Khlebnikov
Silver gilt, enamel
H. 3½ in. (8.9 cm), W. 5¹⁵/₁₆ in. (12.5 cm),
D. 3⅝ in. (9.2 cm)
Hillwood Museum and Gardens, 15.228
Museum purchase 1998

cat. 93

Marks: *kokoshnik* facing right; delta for Moscow; *88*; *Khlebnikov* with imperial warrant

The *kovsh*, an ancient form of a ladle for drinking, was recreated in the late nineteenth century in silver and was often embellished with enamel to transform a once-practical vessel into a decorative object. The handle of this *kovsh* takes the shape of a horse's head. It is also an excellent example of the Khlebnikov firm's ability to turn away from the traditional Russian style and create a *stil modern* form and innovative patterns of enamel.

94. Box

Moscow, ca. 1913
Firm of Fabergé, painting after *The Boyar* by Konstantin Makovskii (1839–1915)
Fedor Rückert (1840–1917), workmaster
Silver gilt, enamel
H. 1¼ in. (3.2 cm), W. 3⅜ in. (8.4 cm),
D. 2⅝ in. (6 cm)
Hillwood Museum and Gardens, 15.209
Museum purchase 1987

Marks: kokoshnik facing right; delta for Moscow; 88; Fabergé in Cyrillic with imperial warrant; inventory number 391831

Rückert was famous for his small enameled paintings on boxes. The matte enamel of this romanticized historical painting contrasts with the high glaze of the stylized borders that frame the miniature.

95. Part of a vodka service

Diatkovo, 1897
Maltsov Glassworks
Elizaveta Bëm (1843–1914), designer
Glass
Decanter (23.497.1–.2): H. 8¹³/₁₆ in. (22.4 cm)
Glasses (23.497.3–.4): H. 3¹/₁₆ in. (8.1 cm)
Hillwood Museum and Gardens
Museum purchase 1997

cat. 95

Inscription in Russian, on front of bottle: *Hello little glasses, how have you been? Have you been waiting for me? Drink, drink, you'll see devils;* left side: *First I don't drink / second I don't want to / third I've already drunk;* back, *We drank, we came to blows! / We slept it off, / and we made up* [cured the hangover with another drink]; right side, *Wine! Yes, my dear? Pour down my throat. O.K. My dear sun!*

On one glass: *Tea, coffee we do not like / as long as there is vodka in the morning;* on the other glass: *One who is quiet while drunk / is not spirited*

Elizaveta Bëm designed a considerable amount of glass for the Maltsov Glassworks at Diatkovo. The firm exhibited some of her glass at the World's Columbian Exposition in Chicago in 1893. Bëm turned to folk imagery seen on green bottle glass made in the eighteenth century for her charming designs on this bottle and glasses.

96. Plate with double-headed eagle

St. Petersburg, 1890s
Factory of the Brothers Kornilov
Hard-paste porcelain
Dia. 9½ in. (24.1 cm)
Private collection

Marks: bear mark designating the factory and underneath in English: *Made in Russia / by Kornilov Bros. / for Bailey, Banks & Biddle / Philadelphia*

The interlace ornament on the border of this plate was extremely popular in the foreign market. The Kornilov Factory employed the double-headed eagle decoratively for popular rather than for imperial use.

97. Bowl

St. Petersburg, 1890s
Factory of Kornilov Brothers
Painting from an illustration by Nikolai Karazin (1842–1908)
Hard-paste porcelain
H. 3 in. (7.6 cm), W. 10 in. (25.4 cm), D. 7¹³/₁₆ in. (19.8 cm)
Private collection

Marks, in Russian: *SPeterburg / Brothers Kornilov / From an original drawing;* signed: *N. Karazin / Reproduction forbidden;* in English: *Made in Russia by Kornilov Bros.*

For the foreign market, the Kornilov Factory typically combined the neo-Byzantine interlace on this bowl's borders with realistic illustrations by Nikolai Karazin.

98. Pair of plates

St. Petersburg, 1890s
Factory of the Brothers Kornilov
Hard-paste porcelain
Dia. 9½ in. (24.1 cm)
Private collection

In Russian: *Brothers Kornilov in S. Peterburg* with imperial warrant

99. Plate and sauce boat

St. Petersburg, 1900–10
Factory of the Brothers Kornilov
Ivan Galnbek (1855–1934), designer
Hard-paste porcelain
Plate: Dia. 9⅝ in. (24.4 cm)
Sauce boat: H. 4⅜ in. (11.1 cm), W. 8⁹/₁₆ in.
(21.7 cm), D. 5¹/₁₆ in. (12.9 cm)
Private collection

Marks on both: bear mark designating the factory; in English: *Made in Russia by Kornilov Brothers*

Inscription on plate: on front, *Tetěrev*; on back, *Moorcock*

On sauceboat: on bottom, *Finch*

Ivan Galnbek, an architect in addition to being a librarian at the Stieglitz School, created designs for the Kornilov Factory. They include a series of tableware with birds, seen here, and others with animals and fish. Galnbek also designed new forms, such as the handle with four indentations. Other handles take the shape of bears, which are often found with ornament designed by the famous illustrator Ivan Bilibin. The mark with the bear was used only for export.

100. Three illustrations from *Volga*

St. Petersburg, 1903
Ivan Bilibin (1876–1942)
Color lithograph
H. 12¼ in. (31.1 cm), W. 14¾ in. (37.5 cm)
Middlebury College Museum of Art, Purchase with funds provided by the Memorial Art Fund, 1994.001

Volga was one of the famous bogatyrs, Russia's legendary warriors, whose feats and adventures are told in this *bylina*, or heroic poem. He would often be transformed into creatures, such as a pike or a mountain goat, to perform his tasks. Although Bilibin more frequently illustrated fairy tales rather than legends, the images of all are characterized by Old Russian landscapes and stylized folk motifs.

101. Costume design for *Le Pavillion d'Armide*, 1909

Alexander Benois (1870–1960)
Watercolor on paper
H. 14¾ in. (37.5 cm), W. 10⅝ in. (27 cm)
The George Riabov Collection of Russian Art,
Jane Voorhees Zimmerli Art Museum,
Rutgers, The State University of New Jersey,
PG 1990.1095

102. Costume design for a gentleman of the court, for *Le Pavillion d'Armide*, 1909

Alexander Benois (1870–1960)
Watercolor on paper
H. 14¾ in. (37.5 cm), W. 10⁷/₁₆ in. (26.5 cm)
The George Riabov Collection of Russian Art,
Jane Voorhees Zimmerli Art Museum,
Rutgers, The State University of New Jersey,
PG 1990.1170

These two costume designs were for the 1909 Ballets Russes production of *Le Pavillion d'Armide*, which was based on Theophile Gautier's story *Omphale* and was performed at the Théâtre du Chatelet in Paris. Nikolai Cherepnin (Tcherepnine) wrote the music, and Michael Fokine choreographed the ballet. Benois designed costumes and sets for the St. Petersburg production at the Mariinskii Theater in 1907. After Sergei Diagilev was denied permission to borrow these sets and costumes, Benois had to recreate them. These two drawings are his second effort.

103. *Ships*, 1917

Anna Ostroumova-Lebedeva (1871–1955)
Color woodcut
H. 10¾ in. (27.2 cm), W. 15¹/₆ in. (38.3 cm)
The George Riabov Collection of Russian Art,
Jane Voorhees Zimmerli Art Museum, Rutgers, The State University of New Jersey,
1994.0352

104. *Ships at Dock*, 1910

Vadim Falileev (1879–1948)
Color woodcut
H. 10¾ in. (27.3 cm), W. 15¹/₆ in. (38.3 cm)
The George Riabov Collection of Russian Art,
Jane Voorhees Zimmerli Collection of Russian Art, Rutgers, The State University of
New Jersey, 1994.0354

SELECTED BIBLIOGRAPHY

Adamson, John, ed. *Princely Courts of Europe: Ritual, Politics and Culture under the Ancien Regime 1500– 1750.* London: Seven Dials, Cassell, 2000.

Alexander, Grand Duke of Russia. *Once a Grand Duke.* New York: Farrar and Rinehart, 1932.

Bing, Edward, ed. *The Secret Letters of the Last Tsar. Being the Confidential Correspondence between Nicholas II and his Mother the Dowager Empress.* New York: Longmans Green and Company, 1938.

Bowlt, John E. *The Silver Age: Russian Art of the Early Twentieth Century and the "World of Art" Group.* Newtonville, Mass.: Oriental Research Partners, 1979.

Buckle, Richard. *Diaghileff.* New York: Atheneum, 1984.

Buxhoeveden, Baroness Sophie. *The Life and Extraordinary Times of Alexandra Feodorovna, Empress of Russia.* London: Longman, Green, 1938; reprint, 1996.

Chachavadze, David. *The Grand Dukes.* New York: Atlantic International Publications, 1990.

Clowes, Edith W., Samuel D. Kassow, and James L. West, eds. *Between Tsar and People. Educated Society and the Quest for Public Identity in Late Imperial Russia.* Princeton: Princeton University Press, 1991.

Cracraft, James. *The Petrine Revolution in Russian Imagery.* Chicago: University of Chicago Press, 1997.

———. *The Petrine Revolution in Russian Architecture.* Chicago: University of Chicago Press, 1988.

George, Grand Duchess. *A Romanov Diary. The Autobiography of H.I. and R.H. Grand Duchess George.* New York: Atlantic International Publications, 1988.

Habsburg, Géza von. *Fabergé.* Geneva: Habsburg, Feldman Editions, 1987.

Habsburg, Géza von, and Marina Lopato. *Fabergé: Imperial Jeweller.* Washington, D.C.: Fabergé Arts Foundation, 1993.

Hughes, Lindsay. *Peter the Great.* New Haven: Yale University Press, 1998.

Kettering, Karen L. *Russian Glass at Hillwood.* Washington, D.C.: Hillwood Museum and Gardens, 2001.

Kirichenko, Evgenia. *Russian Design and the Fine Arts, 1750–1917.* Compiled by Mikhail Anikst. New York: Harry N. Abrams, 1991.

———. "Tsarskoe Selo in the Early Twentieth Century: An Expression of Nicholas II's Idea of Popular Monarchy." In Wendy R. Salmond, ed. *Experiment 7* (2001): 19–71.

Lieven, Dominic. *Nicholas II and the Twilight of the Empire.* New York: St. Martin's Press, 1993.

Maylunas, Andrei, and Sergei Mironenko. *A Lifelong Passion. Nicholas and Alexandra. Their Own Story.* New York: Doubleday, 1997.

Nichols, Robert L. "The Friends of God: Nicholas and Alexandra at the Canonization of Serafim of Sarov, July 1903." In Charles E. Timberlake, ed. *Religious and Secular Forces in Late Tsarist Russia.* Seattle: University of Washington Press, 1992.

———. "The Icon and the Machine in Russia's Religious Renaissance 1900–1909." In William Brumfield and Milos M. Velimirovic, eds. *Christianity and the Arts in Russia.* Cambridge: Cambridge University Press, 1991.

Nicholas and Alexandra. The Last Imperial Family of Tsarist Russia. New York: Harry N. Abrams, 1998.

Nikolai i Aleksandra. Dvor poslednikh russkikh imperatorov. Konets XIX—nachalo XX veka. St. Petersburg: Slaviia–Interbuk, 1994.

Norman, John O. "Alexander III as Patron of Russian Art." In John O. Norman, ed. *New Perspectives on Russian and Soviet Artistic Culture.* New York: St. Martin's Press, 1994.

Odom, Anne. *Fabergé at Hillwood.* Washington, D.C.: Hillwood Museum and Gardens, 1998.

———. "The Politics of Porcelain." In *At the Tsar's Table. From the Raymond F. Piper Collection.* Milwaukee, Wis.: Patrick and Beatrice Haggerty Museum of Art, 2001.

———. *Russian Enamels: From Kievan Rus to Fabergé.* London: Philip Wilson Publishers, 1996.

———. *Russian Imperial Porcelain at Hillwood.* Washington, D.C.: Hillwood Museum and Gardens, 1999.

———. "Russian Patronage and European Culture." In Anne Odom and Liana Paredes Arend. *A Taste for Splendor. Russian Imperial and European Treasures from The Hillwood Museum.* Alexandria, Vir.: Art Services International, 1998.

Romanovsky-Krassinsky, The Princess H.S.H. *Dancing in Petersburg. The Memoirs of Kschessinska.* Garden City, N.Y.: Doubleday and Company, 1961.

Rosenfeld, Alla, ed. *Defining Russian Graphic Arts. 1898–1934. From Diaghilev to Stalin.* Rutgers, N.J.: Rutgers University Press and the Jane Voorhees Zimmerli Art Museum, 1999.

Steinberg, Mark D. "Nicholas and Alexandra: An Intellectual Portrait." In Mark D. Steinberg and Vladimir M. Khrustalëv, eds. *The Fall of the Romanovs: Political Dreams and Personal Struggles in a Time of Revolution.* New Haven: Yale University Press, 1995.

Valkenier, Elizabeth Kridl. *Valentin Serov. Portraits of Russia's Silver Age.* Evanston, Ill.: Northwestern University Press, 2001.

Volkov, Solomon. *St. Petersburg. A Cultural History.* Translated by Antonia W. Bouis. New York: Free Press, 1995.

West, James L., and Iurii A. Petrov, eds. *Merchant Moscow. Images of Russia's Vanished Bourgeoisie.* Princeton: Princeton University Press, 1998.

Wortman, Richard. "Moscow and Petersburg: The Problem of Political Center in Tsarist Russia, 1881–1914." In Sean Wilentz, ed. *Rites of Power: Symbolism, Ritual and Politics since the Middle Ages.* Philadelphia: University of Pennsylvania Press, 1985.

———. *Scenarios of Power: Myth and Ceremony in Russian Monarchy.* Vols. 1 and 2. Princeton: Princeton University Press, 1995 and 2000.

INDEX

cat. 100